SCANDIKITCHEN
FIKA & HYGGE

Comforting cakes and bakes from Scandinavia with love

BRONTË AURELL

Photography by Peter Cassidy

RYLAND PETERS & SMALL
LONDON • NEW YORK

Dedication

For Jonas, Astrid and Elsa – with all my love, always x

Senior Designer
Sonya Nathoo

Editor
Alice Sambrook

Head of Production
Patricia Harrington

Art Director
Leslie Harrington

Editorial Director
Julia Charles

Publisher
Cindy Richards

Food Stylists
Bridget Sargeson,
Jack Sargeson with
Laura Urschel

Assistant Food Stylist
Lola Milne

Prop Stylist
Tony Hutchinson

Recipe Tester
Cathy Seward

Indexer
Vanessa Bird

First published in 2016 by
Ryland Peters & Small
20–21 Jockey's Fields
London WC1R 4BW
and
Ryland Peters & Small, Ltd.
341 E 116th St
New York NY 10029
www.rylandpeters.com

Text © Brontë Aurell 2016

Design and commissioned photographs
© Ryland Peters & Small 2016

ISBN: 978-1-84975-759-1

10 9 8 7 6 5 4 3 2

Printed and bound in Slovenia.

CIP data from the Library of Congress has been applied for.
A CIP record for this book is available from the British Library.

Notes

* Both British (metric) and American (imperial plus US cups) are included in these recipes; however, it is important to work with one set of measurements and not alternate between the two within a recipe.
* All butter should be unsalted unless specified.
* All eggs are medium (UK) or large (US), unless specified as large, in which case US extra large should be used. Uncooked or partially cooked eggs should not be served to the very old, frail, young children, pregnant women or those with compromised immune systems.
* Ovens should be preheated to the specified temperatures. We recommend using an oven thermometer. If using a fan-assisted oven, adjust temperatures according to the manufacturer's instructions.
* When a recipe calls for the grated zest of citrus fruit, buy unwaxed fruit and wash well before using. If you can only find treated fruit, scrub well in warm soapy water before using.

Photography credits

All photography by Peter Cassidy except: 30r Kate Whitaker/Ryland Peters & Small; 38–39 B.Aa. Sætrenes/Getty Images; 48l A house designed by Ilkka Suppanen in Finland. ph Paul Ryan/Ryland Peters & Small; 48r Stella Willing stylist/designer and owner of house in Amsterdam. ph Debi Treloar/Ryland Peters & Small; 49l Nassima Rothacker/Ryland Peters & Small; 49c © Jonathan Birch/Narratives; 49r The home of the designer Stine & Henrik Busk. ph Debi Treloar/Ryland Peters & Small; 58–59 Miriam Glans/Getty Images; 74l Kate Whitaker/Ryland Peters & Small; 74r Johner Images/Getty Images; 75al Kate Whitaker/Ryland Peters & Small; 75c Johner Images/Getty Images; 75r Tim E White/Getty Images; 90–91 Johner Images/Getty Images; 104r Markus Kirchgessner/laif/Camera Press; 105l Steve Painter/Ryland Peters & Small; 105r peder77/Getty Images; 114–115 B.Aa. Sætrenes/Getty Images; 130l The family home of designers Ulla Koskinen & Sameli Rantanen in Finland. ph Debi Treloar/Ryland Peters & Small; 130c & 130r Debi Treloar/Ryland Peters & Small; 131l Hanne Gran's home, Halden, Norway. ph Debi Treloar/Ryland Peters & Small; 138–139 Debi Treloar/Ryland Peters & Small; 158r Steve Painter/Ryland Peters & Small; 159l Johner Images/Getty Images; 172–173 SiriGronskar/Getty Images.

SCANDIKITCHEN
FIKA & HYGGE

CONTENTS

INTRODUCTION

ScandiKitchen, our wonderful café and grocery shop in London's West End, was born out of pure homesickness and a need to find a space where we could meet up with people for a *fika* – a cup of coffee and a bite of something sweet to eat. A place where we could meet with family and friends to just enjoy being together and *hygge* a bit, escaping from the hustle and bustle of day-to-day life. When we first had the idea of opening a Nordic-inspired café almost ten years ago, it was near on impossible to find all the food goodies we missed from home. So we decided to create a place that reflected our love for the foods we missed.

Being Swedish and Danish, it always seemed natural that the concepts of *fika* and *hygge* had to be at the heart of everything we do at the café. One of the first things Jonas made sure was on the menu was the wholesome cinnamon bun – and Brontë even toyed with the idea of naming the café *Hygge* – reflecting just how important this concept is to us. We decided *hygge* might be tricky to pronounce for some, so settled for what we are: a homely Scandinavian kitchen run by a friendly bunch of people. To create a welcoming space was always a priority for us, whether you are a homesick Nordic expat looking for your fix of salty liquorice or anyone else just searching for a nice place for a cup of coffee and a good piece of cake. Anyone can feel a sense of *hygge*, a state of content cosiness with friends where nothing else seems to matter.

Of course, not everybody has the opportunity to just pop by our café to say hello. With this book, we wanted to share some of our favourite autumn and winter treats – perfect for the short, dark winter days. From buns, to cakes, to little pastries – a selection of recipes to make your own traditional *fika* at home and create cosy feelings of *hygge* with people you love. For everybody to be able to bring a bit of Nordic loving to their lives through the cakes we love to make and bake.

In the years since we opened our doors, much has changed about the way Scandinavia is viewed from outside our home countries. Back when we opened, nobody knew the word *fika*, and *hygge* was just another unpronounceable Danish word. Nowadays, books are being written on the concepts of *fika* and *hygge,* and it truly feels as if the world is waking up to the wonders of remembering to turn off the noise from our busy everyday routines. While we're sure they could have done this without Scandinavia's help, having the words to define what we feel is important.

We hope you enjoy this selection of our favourite autumn and winter treats from Scandinavia and that you enjoy creating feelings of *hygge* and *fika* in your own homes.

Brontë & Jonas Aurell

THE SCANDI BAKING PANTRY

Scandinavia is a huge place, so what defines an ingredient as 'local' varies from hilly Norway to flat Denmark - there's a 2,500 km/1,500 mile distance between them. However, we all share a love of lots of similar products, so here is a brief guide to some of the products you will need for Nordic baking. We've put this together based on things we get asked for at the café, and we often help people source specific ingredients or find local replacements to use instead. You will find a more comprehensive list at www.scandikitchen.co.uk.

Popular spices

Caraway/kommen/kummin/karve
In Scandinavia, caraway is known as *kommen*, which sounds similar to 'cumin' so it is often translated incorrectly in recipes. (Cumin is called *spidskommen*.) We use caraway seeds a lot in breads as well as cheeses. In this book it is suggested as a flavouring for crispbread (see page 167).

Cardamom/karemumme/kardemumma
It was actually the Vikings who first sampled this spice during their raids on Constantinople. While we mostly use cardamom in sweet baking and breads, it does occasionally sneak into savoury food (a pinch is used in some regional meatball recipes). It is also sometimes used as a flavouring in strong alcohols.

We use the ground variety, which you can buy in larger supermarkets and Asian speciality shops. I favour using freshly ground cardamom, though, because it is one of those spices that lose potency very quickly when pre-ground. If you use freshly ground, watch the quantity, as it is strong and if you are not used to the punchy flavour, hold back a bit.

To make ground cardamom at home, either buy cardamom seeds online and finely grind in a spice grinder or pestle and mortar, or open the pods (Scandinavians prefer the green pods) and scoop out the seeds to grind (remove the little woody bits of husk inside the pod and only grind the seeds).

Cinnamon/kanel
Where would the Nordic people be without their beloved cinnamon buns? We use cinnamon in a lot of our baking, from biscuits to cakes and breads. There are different grades of cinnamon – go for good-quality ground cinnamon.

Cloves/nelliker/kryddnejlika/nellik
We use both whole cloves and ground cloves in our baking, especially at Christmas, when whole cloves are used in mulled wine and ground cloves are essential in ginger cookies.

Fennel seeds/fennikel frø/fänkålsfrön
We use fennel seeds mainly in bread – both for loaves and as a flavouring for crispbread.

Ginger/ingefær/ingefära
Ground ginger is commonly used in ginger cookies and soft ginger cake, but also in some other cakes. Whole dried ginger is essential in mulled wine.

Liquorice/lakrids/lakrits
While we have a long history full of love for liquorice, it is only in recent years we have started to bake with it. This is largely due to great brands of purist liquorice coming to the market, such as Lakrids by Bülow from Denmark and Lakritsfabrikken in Sweden. Either the powder or liquorice syrup is used in most sweet recipes. In some Swedish recipes it can be referred to as Hockey Pulver.

Salt
The Nordics have been preserving food in salt for centuries and we love salty foods, both

savoury and sweet. We add salt to many cookies and cakes and we love salty liquorice. We use ammonium chloride for flavouring our liquorice, also known as *salmiakki*. It is an acquired taste – but once you get the taste for things such as salty liquorice, a life-long addiction usually starts. You have been warned.

Saffron/safran/saffran

People In Sweden and Norway use saffron during the month of December in traditional Lucia buns. We commonly use ground saffron, which you can buy in specialist shops (ask behind the counter, as they are usually kept behind the till). If you are using strands, grind these before use. To intensify the colour, soak in warm liquid before using.

Seville orange peel/pomerans

We use this in our mulled wine and dried in some Christmas breads and biscuits. You can substitute with normal dried orange peel, but the flavour will not be as subtle or bitter.

Vanilla/vanilje/vanilj

Scandinavian recipes often call for vanilla sugar, which is a quick and easy substitute for whole vanilla pod/beans. You can make your own at home by adding 250 g/1 cup of icing/confectioners' sugar to a food processor or spice grinder with two vanilla pods/beans – dried out hard ones are fine – a great way to use these up. Pulse until pulverized, then sift out the large pieces of peel. You can buy vanilla sugar in any Scandinavian food shops, too – Tørsleff is a great brand. You can, of course, also always substitute with vanilla extract or real vanilla pods/beans.

Berries

Cloudberries/multebær/hjortron

Fresh cloudberries are rare. They grow wild near the Arctic Circle and their season lasts around three weeks in July and August. They are hard to cultivate and foragers don't tend to part with

information freely! Frozen cloudberries are easier to get hold of but they are expensive. A little goes a long way; this is a gourmet berry, even to the Scandinavians. Most Scandinavian shops will stock cloudberry jam, which can be used in most of our baking recipes. The cloudberry is very tart and the jam/jelly is not used as a spread for toast, as it is far too expensive. Use it with strong cheese or in desserts (it's particularly great heated up and poured over vanilla ice cream). To replace this flavour in recipes is hard.

Lingonberries/tyttebær/lingon

Norwegians, Finns and Swedes will have lingonberries in their freezers throughout the year; fresh ones are picked in August. We also have lingonberry jam/jelly and compotes in our store cupboards. You can use the frozen or fresh berries for baking, and you can also use the jam for some cakes or cookies. If you cannot get hold of lingonberries, substitute with cranberries or raspberries, depending on the recipe. Many Scandinavian shops sell the frozen berries.

Grains and flours

Oats/havregryn

Used in porridge, granola, muesli and baking. We also eat raw oats with milk for breakfast. Oat flakes (jumbo oats) or cut oats are favoured.

Potato flour/kartoffelmel/potatismjöl/potetmel

You can buy this in speciality stores. Once potato starch is added, the dish should not boil (especially in fruit-based sauces as these will go cloudy after boiling).

Rye flour rugmel/rågmjöl

There are two kinds of rye flour sold in supermarkets. Wholegrain dark rye and light (sifted) rye. Light rye flour is often called Type 997. It is, basically, sifted wholegrain rye flour, so if you are pushed, you can sift the dark rye flour before using in a recipe.

Rye flour mix/sigtemel/rågsikt

In Sweden and Denmark, rågsikt (sigtemel in Danish) is very common. It's 60% white wheat flour and 40% light rye (type 997), sifted. You can make this at home by mixing the same quantities.

Rye flakes/rugflager/rågflingor

I love using rye flakes in granola, flapjacks and porridge (mixed with normal oats) for their nutty flavour and good bite. Available in health-food stores, they take longer to cook and are quite chewy. If you are using oats in a recipe, consider mixing part oats, part rye flakes.

Semolina/semuljegryn/mannagryn/semulegryn

Used for some desserts and also as a porridge.

Spelt flour/speltmel/dinkelmjöl

This is an older type of wheat grain and less refined. You can get both white and wholegrain spelt flour – we use both in this book. Spelt contains less gluten than other wheat flours.

Yeast and leaveners

Baker's ammonia/hartshorn powder/hjortetakssalt/hjorthornssalt

Used in old Nordic recipes to ensure cookies rise and get crispy at lower temperatures, baker's ammonia gives off a very strong ammonia smell as you bake, but this disappears as soon as the cookies cool.

You can buy it online or at some pharmacies, as well as in many Scandinavian food shops. It was traditionally made from the ground antlers of young stags, but nowadays it's all chemical. When using baker's ammonia, don't eat the raw dough. Substitute with baking powder, although the result will not be as crispy.

Dry active yeast

Little yeast granules you have to activate in lukewarm water before using. This is the next best thing to fresh yeast. Activate and leave for 15 minutes in the finger-warm liquid to go frothy and bubbly – then use in the recipe as normal.

Fresh yeast

25 g/1 oz. of fresh yeast (also known as compressed yeast) is the equivalent to 13 g/$^{1}/_{2}$ oz. of dry active yeast. It usually comes in packs of 50 g/2 oz. and looks a bit like clay. Take care not to kill fresh yeast with hot liquid or by adding salt to the yeast before the flour.

If you use heavier flours, such as rye, the yeast takes a long time to lift it and you will have denser breads. Consider mixing lighter flours with the darker ones if you want fluffy loaves.

Instant dried yeast

If you have no option but to use instant dry yeast (a fine powder sold in sachets), skip the adding to liquid step and add to the dry ingredients. Follow the manufacturer's guidelines for equivalent measures.

Other stuff

Marzipan/marsipan

We use ready-made marzipan in a lot of our baking recipes and have included an easy recipe to make your own 50/50 marzipan (see page 15). In the UK and America, marzipan is commonly only 25% almonds.

You can bind marzipan with water instead of egg white if you are worried about eating raw egg, but I think egg whites make it smooth and easier to work with. However, leftover marzipan bound with water will keep in the fridge a little longer.

Punch

A type of Swedish rum liqueur often used to flavour rum truffle treats such as Romkugler (see page 56) – you can substitute with good concentrated rum flavourings for baked treats if you prefer.

BASIC RECIPES

These basic recipes are referred to in various recipes throughout the book. They are good staples and can be mixed and matched with other ingredients of your choosing – once you have exhausted the delicious options in this book, of course! Be sure to double-check whether to use the full amount or half the quantity listed here.

LAYER CAKE BASES

This base for layer cakes is similar to a very light Genoise sponge. You can, of course, bake these in three pans to make them uniform, but I find it just as easy to draw circles on baking parchment and then cut the edges to fit once baked. Some people use baking powder in layer cakes but I usually opt to use just eggs and sugar as the leavener because I feel the end result is more delicate. However, it can be trickier. The secret is to whip the eggs and sugar properly to ribbon stage – this can take several minutes to achieve. Secondly, when you fold in the flour, do so very gently in figure-of-eight folds and don't rush it.

25 g/¼ stick butter, melted
and set aside to cool

4 eggs

120 g/²/₃ cup caster/granulated sugar

120 g/²/₃ cup plus 2 tablespoons plain/
all-purpose flour or cake flour

a pinch of salt

1 teaspoon vanilla sugar OR extract
OR use the seeds of 1 vanilla pod/bean

*3 baking sheets, greased and lined
with baking parchment*

Preheat the oven to 180°C (350°F) Gas 4.

Beat together the eggs and sugar on high speed in a stand mixer or using a hand-held electric whisk. Beat until the mixture reaches ribbon stage – you will be able to see the traces of the mixture when you move the whisk.

Use a 20-cm/8-inch diameter plate to draw three circles on baking parchment. Cut these out and place one parchment circle on each of the three baking sheets. Set aside.

Combine the flour, salt and vanilla in a separate bowl. Sift into the egg mixture, bit by bit, carefully folding using a figure-of-eight movement until incorporated. Pour the cooled melted butter down the side of the bowl and fold carefully again, trying not to knock out air.

Divide the mixture evenly between the parchment circles on the baking sheets spreading right to the edges of each circle with the back of a spoon. If they go over a bit, don't worry, you can cut these bits off afterwards.

Bake in the preheated oven for about 5–7 minutes or until light golden brown.

Remove from the oven and allow to cool completely before removing the baking parchment. If the parchment sticks, slightly dampen the paper side with cold water and the paper will come off easily. Trim any untidy edges using a sharp knife.

Note: If you really want to use baking powder, add 1 teaspoon to the flour for a slight lift.

DANISH PASTRY

Many people are scared to attempt Danish pastry from scratch. It is, admittedly, a little time-consuming, but it isn't actually hard – it is so worth it once you taste those flaky pastries, straight from the oven. Originally, Viennese pastry (Vienna bread or *Wienerbrød*) was brought to Denmark by Austrian bakers around 1850, and the Danish variety developed from there.

25 g/1 oz. fresh yeast or 13 g/$2^{1}/2$ teaspoons dried/active dry yeast

150 ml/$^{2}/3$ cup whole milk, heated to 36–37°C (97–98°F)

50 g/$^{1}/4$ cup caster/granulated sugar

50 g/$3^{1}/2$ tablespoons butter, softened

350 g/$2^{1}/2$ cups strong white/bread flour, plus extra for dusting

1 teaspoon salt

1 egg plus 1 yolk

FILLING:

350 g/3 sticks butter, softened

25 g/3 tablespoons plain/all-purpose flour

a baking sheet, lined with baking parchment

If you are using fresh yeast, add the yeast and whole milk to a stand mixer with a dough hook attached. Mix until the yeast has dissolved.

If using dried/active dry yeast, pour the milk into a bowl, sprinkle over the yeast and whisk together. Cover with clingfilm/plastic wrap and leave in a warm place for about 15 minutes to activate and become frothy and bubbly. Pour into the mixer with the dough hook attached.

Stir in the sugar and softened butter, then mix the flour with the salt and start to add, bit by bit. Add the egg halfway through along with the remaining flour. Keep mixing with the dough hook for a good 5 minutes. The resulting dough should still be a little bit sticky.

Cover the bowl with clingfilm/plastic wrap and leave to rise for an hour or until doubled in size.

Turn the dough out onto a floured surface and knead through, adding more flour as needed until you have a stretchy, workable dough. Roll the dough out into a big square 35 x 35 cm/14 x 14 inches or as evenly as you can.

For the filling, mix the butter with the flour into a just mouldable ball using your hands. It's important this mixture ends up being a similar consistency to the dough – this will make it easier to roll. If your hands are too warm, use a rolling pin and beat the butter flat between two sheets of baking parchment. Flatten the butter out to a square around 25 x 25 cm/$9^{3}/4$ x $9^{3}/4$ inches then place this butter square onto your dough at a 45 degree angle so that the dough corners can fold back in to cover the butter, like an envelope.

Carefully fold the dough corners over the butter until you have completely enclosed it. Dust with flour and carefully roll out the package to a rectangle around 30 x 50 cm/$11^{3}/4$ x 20 inches then fold the layers the short way twice so you end up with a rectangle approx 30 x 15 cm/$11^{3}/4$ x 6 inch (3 layers with butter). It is important that you roll carefully so that the butter stays inside the pastry package.

Place the dough on the prepared baking sheet, cover with clingfilm/plastic wrap and chill for 15 minutes in the refrigerator. Repeat the folding process: roll to a rectangle and fold back on itself – you now have 9 layers of butter. Again, rest the dough in the fridge for 15 minutes, then repeat the rolling process again so you end up with yet another rectangle in 3 folds with 27 layers of butter in total. After a final rest in the refrigerator, your pastry is now ready to shape into whatever you want to bake.

At any stage during the making of Danish pastries, if your hands or the dough get too warm, step back and cool things down a bit, as this can spoil your end result.

SWEET SHORTCRUST PASTRY

This basic sweet shortcrust pastry is useful for many recipes in this book. If you prefer a less sweet base, simply reduce the sugar content slightly. Remember that keeping the butter as cold as possible is key to making pastry with a good short texture.

200 g/1¾ sticks cold butter, cubed
350 g/2⅔ cups plain/all-purpose flour
125 g/1 cup plus 1 tablespoon icing/confectioners' sugar
1 teaspoon vanilla extract OR seeds from half a vanilla pod/bean
1 egg

MAKES 700 G/1½ LB. DOUGH

Rub the cold butter into the plain/all-purpose flour until sandy in texture, then add the icing/confectioners' sugar and vanilla. Add the whole egg and mix until the dough holds together and becomes smooth, taking care not to over-mix. You can also make the dough in the food processor by pulsing the ingredients together briefly, if you wish.

Wrap the dough in clingfilm/plastic wrap and chill for at least 30 minutes in the refrigerator before using.

PASTRY CREAM

There is something so deliciously decadent about cakes with pastry cream. The comfort of custard, I usually call it. I love making it from scratch and use it for anything from filling cakes to layering trifles and serving it with crumbles (for that, I simply thin with a bit of milk). The only thing to watch out for is not to burn the milk, as this will spoil the whole lot.

500 ml/2 cups whole milk
1 vanilla pod/bean, seeds scraped
1 whole egg plus 1 egg yolk
100 g/½ cup caster/superfine sugar
30 g/¼ cup cornflour/cornstarch
½ teaspoon salt
25 g/2 tablespoons butter

MAKES APPROX. 600–625 G/21–22 OZ.

In a saucepan, heat the milk with the scraped out seeds from the vanilla pod/bean.

In a separate bowl, whisk together the eggs and sugar and add the cornflour/cornstarch.

When the milk has just reached boiling point, take off the heat and pour one third into the egg mixture while whisking continuously.

Once whisked through, pour the egg mixture back into the remaining hot milk. Return to the stove and bring to the boil, carefully. Whisk continuously as the mixture thickens, for just under a minute, then remove from the heat and stir in the salt and butter.

Pour into a cold bowl and place a sheet of baking parchment on top to prevent the cream from forming a crust as it cools. The mixture will keep well in the refrigerator for a few days.

MARZIPAN (FOR BAKING)

I love baking with marzipan – from *Kransekage* to Mazarin Tart and even Lent Buns, a good 50/50 marzipan has many uses. If you buy marzipan in most UK supermarkets, you will get 25% almond and 75% sugar – but in Scandinavian baking, we use 50% almond for baking and 60% almond for petits fours and finer cakes. This is such a simple way to make marzipan. I use egg white to bind – which means that it won't keep as long, so make only what you need.

200 g/2 cups finely ground almonds (if the grind feels a bit coarse, re-grind it at home a few times in your grinder or processor)
100 g/^{1}/2 cup caster/granulated sugar
100 g/^{2}/3 cup icing/confectioners' sugar
1 teaspoon almond extract
1 medium egg white (approx. 30 g/1 oz.) ideally pasteurized

MAKES APPROX. 400 G/14 OZ.

Blend the ingredients together in a food processor until you have a smooth marzipan.

Roll the mixture into a log and wrap tightly in clingfilm/plastic wrap. Chill in the refrigerator for at least 1 hour before using.

REMONCE ALMOND PASTE

This is a classic almond-based filling for Danish pastries. It is nearly always baked rather than used raw and is integral to many Nordic cake and pastry recipes. Sometimes, cinnamon, vanilla and dark brown sugar are added (for cinnamon swirls and buns, for example). Remonce is sometimes translated to Lord Mayor's filling, although I've never heard this term used in the UK, so I wonder if this translation perhaps stems from the filling used in *Borgmesterkringle* – the name meaning 'Mayor's Kringle'.

100 g/3^1/2 oz. marzipan (minimum 50% store-bought or see recipe above)
100 g/7 tablespoons butter, softened
100 g/^{3}/4 cup plus 1^1/2 tablespoons icing/ confectioners' sugar, sifted

MAKES APPROX. 300 G/10^1/2 OZ.

Grate the marzipan into a bowl.

Add the softened butter and icing/confectioners' sugar.

Whisk everything together until smooth. Your remonce paste is now ready to use.

BISCUITS
& COOKIES

In Scandinavia, anything small and baked in the fashion
of a biscuit or cookie is called a little cake (*småkage* in Danish),
which I guess is what it is. A perfect two bites with a cup of tea
or coffee. Throughout Scandinavia, you will find hundreds
of recipes for different varieties – too many to include here. We
have chosen some favourites from our café to share with you.

Kokostoppe
COCONUT TOPS

These super-easy treats are the Scandinavian version of the coconut macaroon. They are gloriously soft and sticky – and gluten-free, too. You can make endless flavour variations: classic vanilla or filled with berries or spices. Personally, I love to add cardamom or lime zest.

3 egg whites

a pinch of salt

200 g/1 cup caster/ granulated sugar

200 g/2 cups desiccated/ dried shredded coconut

50 g/¹/₂ cup ground almonds

1 teaspoon vanilla extract

50–100 g/2–3¹/₂ oz. dark/ bittersweet chocolate, chopped, to coat the bases

flavouring of your choice (see method)

2 baking sheets, greased and lined with baking parchment

MAKES 18–20

Beat the egg whites and salt until soft peaks form using a hand-held electric whisk or in a stand mixer with the whisk attachment. In a separate bowl combine the caster/granulated sugar, desiccated/dried shredded coconut and ground almonds. Fold into the egg whites with the vanilla extract until you have a thick mass, taking care not to knock out the air. Add your choice of flavouring (see flavour options below).

Leave the mixture to rest in the refrigerator for 15–20 minutes; this will make it easier to mould.

Preheat the oven to 175°C (350°F) Gas 4.

Divide and shape the chilled mixture into rough 'tops' or little mounds of around 25 g/1 oz. each in weight. You could also make log shapes or firmer round shapes, I prefer the more rustic look.

Bake in the preheated oven for 8–12 minutes, depending on the size of the tops and strength of your oven. Keep a close eye on the tops, as they will brown quickly and can burn. They are done when slightly golden all over. Leave to cool on a wire rack.

To decorate, melt half the chocolate in a heatproof bowl set over a pan of barely simmering water. Do not let the base of the bowl touch the water. Remove from the heat and add the other half of the chocolate immediately, stirring in well. Wait a minute or two until all the chocolate has melted, then dip the base of each coconut top into the chocolate and leave on their side on a plate or tray for the chocolate to cool.

Flavour options: zest from 1 lime + 3 tablespoons fresh OR frozen raspberries OR lingonberries, lightly crushed OR 1 teaspoon ground cardamom.

Daimkakor
DAIM COOKIES

A good cookie recipe is essential to a complete baking repertoire. These are wonderfully gooey and filled with pieces of delicious chocolate-coated almond toffee. Daim is one of the most popular chocolate bars in Sweden. It originated in Scandinavia during the fifties and was then bought by Kraft foods and renamed Dime. Now it's back to being Daim again – and remains a Nordic favourite. You can use another type of chocolate bar if you can't get hold of Daim.

150 g/1¼ sticks butter

300 g/2 cups plus 2 tablespoons plain/all-purpose flour

½ teaspoon bicarbonate of/baking soda

½ teaspoon vanilla sugar OR extract OR the seeds from 1 vanilla pod/bean

¼ teaspoon sea salt

150 g/¾ cup light brown soft sugar

100 g/½ cup caster/granulated sugar

1 egg

1 egg yolk

2 tablespoons whole milk

5 Daim bars (each weighing 28 g/1 oz.), roughly chopped

2 baking sheets, greased and lined with baking parchment

MAKES 20-22 COOKIES (DEPENDING ON HOW MUCH DOUGH YOU EAT!)

Melt the butter and set aside to cool down.

Combine flour, bicarbonate of/baking soda, vanilla and salt in a bowl and set side.

Combine the sugars with the cooled, melted butter and stir until no lumps remain. Combine the egg, egg yolk and milk and mix with the sugar and butter until thoroughly combined.

Add the flour, bit by bit, mixing until everything is incorporated. Add the Daim pieces and mix to combine. Wrap the dough in clingfilm/plastic wrap and place in the refrigerator to chill for a few hours.

Preheat the oven to 190°C (375°F) Gas 5.

Form the dough into rough balls, each weighing about 40 g/1½ oz. and place on the prepared baking sheets around 5 cm/2 inches apart.

Bake in the preheated oven for 8–10 minutes or until just golden. Remove from the oven immediately and transfer to a cooling rack – the middle should still be slightly soft but they will harden up after a while. The cookies will be at their very best about half an hour after removing from the oven, when they are still slightly warm and beautifully chewy in the middle.

Ingenting

NOTHING BISCUITS

This treat is called *Ingenting* – which means 'nothing'. Because when people say 'I can eat nothing more', you can always fit in one of these very light treats!

BISCUIT BASES:
300 g/2¼ cups plain/all-purpose flour
2 egg yolks
175 g/1½ sticks butter
2 tablespoons double/heavy cream
25 g/1 oz. icing/confectioners' sugar
½ teaspoon grated lemon zest

MERINGUE TOPPING:
2 egg whites
a tiny pinch of salt
275 g/1½ cups minus 2 tablespoons caster/superfine sugar

1 teaspoon vanilla sugar OR extract OR the seeds from 1 vanilla pod/bean
1 teaspoon white wine vinegar
3 tablespoons finely chopped almonds

a baking sheet, greased and lined with baking parchment

a 5-cm/1-inch fluted pastry/cookie cutter

a piping/pastry bag fitted with a star nozzle/tip

MAKES 30–35

Blitz the ingredients for the biscuit bases briefly in a food processor. Once a smooth dough has formed, wrap in clingfilm/plastic wrap and chill in the refrigerator for at least 30 minutes.

Preheat the oven to 160°C (300°F) Gas 2.

Roll out the dough on a lightly floured surface to a thickness of 3 mm/⅛ inch. Use the round fluted pastry/cookie cutter to stamp out circles and place on the prepared baking sheet. Repeat until all the dough has been used.

For the meringue topping, beat the egg whites with a tiny pinch of salt until stiff using a hand-held electric whisk or in a stand mixer with the whisk attachment. Slowly add the sugar and vanilla, bit by bit, and whisk on high speed until you have a shiny mixture that forms stiff peaks (still soft enough to be spoon-able). Fold in the vinegar and chopped almonds.

Pipe or spoon the meringue mixture onto each biscuit base, spreading or placing almost to the edge (the meringue will not spread much during baking).

Bake the biscuits in the middle of the preheated oven for around 18–20 minutes or until the base is cooked and the top is lightly browned. Remove from the oven and allow to cool before eating.

Jødekager
JEWISH BISCUITS

I remember my grandmother in Denmark making these when I was very little. I loved the smell of the cinnamon as they baked and I remember pacing by the oven impatiently, waiting for the goodies to cool down enough so I could get my grubby little fingers on them. The name *Jødekager* means, literally, Jewish biscuits. This name stems from the 1800s when Eastern European Jews settled in Copenhagen, and many sold baked goods for a living. This biscuit is particularly popular around Christmas time in Denmark, but I've always wondered why it isn't made all year round – it's deliciously light and crispy, and super-easy to make.

175 g/1^1/$_2$ sticks cold butter, cubed

200 g/1^1/$_2$ cups plain/all-purpose flour

^{1}/$_2$ teaspoon baking powder

100 g/^{1}/$_2$ cup caster/granulated sugar

1 egg yolk

TOPPING:

1 egg white

2 teaspoons ground cinnamon

2 tablespoons caster/granulated sugar

small handful chopped almonds

2–3 baking sheets, greased and lined with baking parchment

MAKES APPROX. 40

Combine the cold cubed butter with the plain/all-purpose flour and baking powder in a stand mixer with the paddle attachment or in a food processor. Mix briefly until you have a grainy, sand-like texture. Add the caster/granulated sugar and egg yolk and mix until the ingredients are just evenly incorporated.

Roll the dough into a neat log (about 5 cm/2 inches in diameter) and wrap in clingfilm/plastic wrap. Chill in the refrigerator for at least an hour, but ideally longer (overnight is good).

Preheat the oven to 180°C (350°F) Gas 4.

Using a sharp knife, carefully slice your pastry log into thin slices. Place the dough slices on the prepared baking sheets. Try not to handle them too much – they bake more evenly if they stay cold.

Brush each piece of dough with a little egg white using a pastry brush. Mix together the cinnamon and caster/granulated sugar and scatter over the biscuits/cookies. Add a small sprinkling of chopped almonds to the middle of each.

Bake in the preheated oven for around 10–12 minutes or until the biscuits/cookies start to brown at the edges. Be aware that these biscuits burn easily, so keep a sharp eye on them. They need to be taken out of the oven before they brown all over.

Leave the biscuits/cookies on a wire rack to cool and crisp up before eating.

Apelsinpepparkakor
NORDIC ORANGE AND GINGER BISCUITS

At Christmas time all over Scandinavia a mountain of ginger cookies are consumed at festive get-togethers and *fika* breaks. This version is super-traditional, with the added zing of orange zest.

550 g/4 cups plain/all-purpose flour
1 teaspoon bicarbonate of/baking soda
1 teaspoon ground ginger
1 teaspoon ground cloves
2 teaspoons ground cinnamon
1 teaspoon ground cardamom
a pinch of ground all-spice
a pinch of salt
150 g/1 stick plus 2 tablespoons butter, room temperature
zest of 1 orange

200 g/10 tablespoons golden/light corn syrup
100 g/^{1}/2 cup caster/granulated sugar
100 g/^{1}/2 cup dark brown soft sugar
150 ml/^{1}/2 cup double/heavy cream
icing/confectioners' sugar, to dust

2 or more baking sheets, greased and lined with baking parchment

festive shaped pastry/cookie cutters

MAKES 50–70

Mix the flour and bicarbonate of/baking soda with the dry spices and salt.

Add the butter and all the other ingredients and mix until you have an even dough. It may still be sticky, but shape into a log and wrap in clingfilm/plastic wrap and leave to rest in the refrigerator overnight before using. Try to resist eating the dough every time you pass by the fridge. Yes, we know it is hard not to do!

Preheat the oven to 200°C (400°F) Gas 6.

Roll out the dough thinly on a lightly floured work surface and use cookie cutters to cut your desired shapes. You want the biscuits/cookies to be thin.

Place on the prepared baking sheets and bake in the preheated oven for 5–6 minutes or until the biscuits/cookies turn a darker shade of brown. This is a large quantity of dough so you may need to bake the biscuits in batches.

Remove from the oven and cool on a wire rack. Store in an airtight container or serve dusted with icing/confectioners' sugar.

Pebernødder
'PEPPER NUTS' OR DANISH CHRISTMAS BISCUITS

These biscuits are essential at the lead-up to Christmas in Danish households. Some say they are truly of Danish origin, among the first biscuits baked here in the Middle Ages. Others say the recipe travelled up via Holland and Germany. There are no nuts in the dough – the name simply refers to the shape of a small nut. Back in the day, to 'pepper something' meant to spice it up; this is now more symbolic, but I still like a subtle amount of white pepper in mine.

200 g/1¾ sticks butter
200 g/1 cup caster/granulated sugar
425 g/3¼ cups plain/all-purpose flour
1 teaspoon baking powder
1 teaspoon bicarbonate of/baking soda
a pinch of salt
75 ml/⅓ cup double/heavy cream

SPICE MIX:
½ teaspoon ground white pepper
1 teaspoon mixed spice/apple pie spice
2 teaspoons ground cinnamon
1 teaspoon ground cardamom
½ teaspoon ground ginger
½ teaspoon ground cloves

2 baking sheets, greased and lined with baking parchment

MAKES 100–120

Combine the spices for the spice mix in a small bowl.

In a separate bowl, cream together the butter and caster/granulated sugar until pale and fluffy using a hand-held electric whisk or balloon whisk. Add the spice mix and sift in the plain/all-purpose flour, baking powder, bicarbonate of/baking soda and salt. Finally, add the double/heavy cream. Mix until you have an even dough. Wrap the dough in clingfilm/plastic wrap and leave to chill for 30 minutes in the refrigerator.

Preheat the oven to 200°C (400°F) Gas 6.

Roll the dough into little balls of around 5–6 g/¼ oz. each. Arrange on the prepared baking sheets. The dough will spread only slightly when baked, so you should be able to fit many on each sheet. (This dough should be enough to make over a hundred; it sounds a lot but they are small and get eaten quickly!)

Bake in the preheated oven for 8–10 minutes or until golden. Leave to cool on a wire rack. The pepper nuts will crisp up nicely as they cool down. Store in an airtight container.

Seven kinds of biscuits

Back in 1945, as Europe emerged from war, a book called *Sju Sorters Kakor* was published in Sweden. The title means 'seven kinds of biscuits' – a reference to the amount of varieties of biscuit or cookie that the lady of the house would be expected to offer to her guests. That didn't include additional buns, cakes or breads, either!

Sju Sorters Kakor was a cookbook put together with suggestions from households all over Sweden and over 8,000 recipes were initially submitted. It ended up containing around 300 traditional recipes and quickly became a bestseller. It is now in its 84th edition and every household in Sweden owns at least two copies. This average only increases year by year, because nobody would ever dare to throw out any of the older handed-down copies. (I have five passed down from various great aunts – if you want a copy, let me know.)

These days, very few households stay up late to bake seven kinds of cookies just because the neighbours are coming over for *fika*, but the concept dates back to the late 1800s when, after a period of prohibition, people were once again allowed to drink coffee, and to meet up and do so became something of an occasion. Those households who could offer the finest variety of baked goods along with their coffee were considered superior, and the fashion for elaborate *kafferep* (coffee parties for ladies) soon spread. Although seven varieties was the minimum to

offer, if anyone went beyond that, it might have been considered pompous. This concept of having just enough (not too much, not too little) is known as *lagom* and can be applied to almost every aspect of life in Sweden.

Towards the end of the 19th century, in the Sønderborg area of Denmark, the Second Schleswig War of 1864 meant that the region was under German rule. During this time, people were forbidden to meet and consume alcohol in taverns, but they were allowed to meet in community houses. Ladies would bring elaborate cakes and the famous *kaffebord* (cake tables) became bigger and better. During the Second World War, the tradition for elaborate cakes again became popular, as the only public meetings allowed during occupation were for coffee and cake. Under the guise of eating cake, resistance matters could be discussed.

On a traditional *Sønderjysk kaffebord* (Southern Jutland coffee table), there are seven types of cookies and seven kinds of soft cake. There are strict rules on how to approach such an offering: first, one would start with a good *bundlag* (base layer) of wheat buns with lots of butter. From there, one would go from the soft cakes to the harder ones: from cream cakes to the drier

varieties and finishing up with biscuits/cookies. Traditionally, guests were expected to take slices of everything and keep them in front of them on several plates. To refuse anything would have been seen as an insult to the baker.

Elaborate and lengthy coffee table meetings in Denmark were not only reserved for discussions of war. Local gatherings were held to discuss important village matters, too. Personally, I can't think of a better way to settle disagreements (whether large or small) than over copious amounts of coffee and cake – there are few people who cannot be reasoned with after a bucket load of whipped cream.

The *Sønderjysk kaffebord* is a wonderful part of Danish food heritage. During the 1960s, it all but disappeared, but today it has been revived. You can find Southern Jutland coffee tables at fancy cafés and hotels all over the region as well as at larger celebrations. If you are in the area, it is worth seeking one out. Just remember not to eat breakfast before you go!

Hallongrottor
SMALL RASPBERRY TREATS

This is one of the most iconic bakes for the Swedish fika table. *Hallongrottor* are included in every grandma's baking book, and are one of the first treats we learn to bake. Kids just love them – and why wouldn't they? A crumbly vanilla biscuit/cookie with fruity jam/jelly is always a winner.

250 g/2¼ sticks butter, cubed
1 teaspoon grated lime zest
200 g/1½ cups plain/all-purpose flour
80 g/¾ cup cornflour/cornstarch
2 teaspoons vanilla sugar OR extract OR the seeds from 1 vanilla pod/bean
75 g/½ cup plus ½ tablespoon icing/confectioners' sugar
1 teaspoon baking powder
a pinch of salt

150 g/½ cup high fruit content raspberry jam/jelly (or flavour of your choosing)
flaked/slivered almonds and extra icing/confectioners' sugar, to decorate

a muffin pan, lined with paper cases or a mini muffin pan, lined with petit four cases

a piping/pastry bag fitted with a plain nozzle/tip

MAKES 20 LARGE OR 35 SMALL

Preheat the oven to 180°C (350°F) Gas 4.

In a stand mixer with the paddle attachment or in a food processor, combine the butter and lime zest with the dry ingredients (plain/all-purpose flour, cornflour/cornstarch, vanilla sugar, icing/confectioners' sugar, baking powder and salt), stopping when you have a smooth, even dough. Try not to overwork the dough.

Form the dough into a sausage shape. Cut the dough either into 15 g/½ oz. or 25 g /1 oz. pieces and roll into balls. Place the balls into the paper cases in the prepared muffin pan or mini muffin pan.

Press each ball in the middle using your thumb to make a deep hole for the jam/jelly. Use a piping/pastry bag to fill each hole with your chosen jam (1 large teaspoon per hole for the large ones or ½ teaspoon for the small ones). Add slivered/flaked almonds on top.

Bake in the preheated oven for 15–20 minutes or until slightly golden in colour. Remove from the oven and leave to cool on a wire rack. Remove the paper cases before arranging on a pretty plate or cake stand and dusting with icing/confectioners' sugar to serve. Keeps well in an airtight container for 2–3 days.

Vaniljekranse
DANISH VANILLA COOKIES

Around the world, people buy Danish butter cookies in pretty tins, but those biscuits taste nothing like the home-made version. While writing this book, I had many discussions with friends about how to recreate a recipe that tasted 'just like Grandma's', and found that it was harder than I first thought. Truth be told, nothing can replace the taste of those biscuits that she made – there was so much love in them, heaven and earth together can't find a substitution. Still, after much trying, these do taste almost like my *Mormor* Erna's did. I hope that one day, my grandkids will bake these and say they taste just like Grandma Brontë's.

1 whole vanilla pod/bean

250 g /1¼ cups caster/granulated sugar

250 g/2¼ sticks cold butter, cubed

325 g/scant 2½ cups plain/all-purpose flour

a pinch of salt

1 teaspoon baking powder

75 g/⅔ cup ground almonds

1 egg

50 g/¼ cup finely chopped almonds

3-4 baking sheets, greased and lined with baking parchment

a strong, fabric piping/pastry bag fitted with a large star nozzle/tip

MAKES 40

Grind the whole vanilla pod/bean, including the skin, with 3 tablespoons of the caster/granulated sugar in a spice grinder or food processor. Sift out any big lumps and set aside.

In a stand mixer or food processor, combine the cold butter with the plain/all-purpose flour, a pinch of salt, baking powder and the vanilla sugar mixture. Mix with the paddle attachment or pulse briefly, until the mixture has a coarse, sandy texture.

Add the ground almonds and remaining caster/granulated sugar and mix again, then add the egg and chopped almonds. Mix until you have an even dough that is soft enough to push through a piping/pastry bag. Note: you will need a strong fabric piping bag for this and a larger nozzle as the dough is really, really hard to push out. It may help to warm the dough with your hands until mouldable. Alternatively, you can also simply roll these, but they will not have the pattern.

Pipe (or roll) the dough into 8-10 cm/3¼-4 inch long sausages. Carefully connect the two ends of each to form rings and place on the prepared baking sheets. Make sure the dough is no thicker than the width of your little finger, because these will spread during baking.

Chill the dough rings on the baking sheets in the refrigerator for at least 30 minutes. This will help the biscuits to keep their piped pattern as they bake.

Preheat the oven to 200°C (400°F) Gas 6.

Pop the cold tray into the preheated oven and bake the biscuits for 8-10 minutes, or until the edges are just slightly tinged golden brown. Remove from the oven and allow to cool and harden before eating. Store in an airtight container as the biscuits do go soft quickly.

Drömmar

SWEDISH 'DREAM' BISCUITS

There are many traditional Scandinavian biscuits that use baker's ammonia (ammonium carbonate) as a leavening agent instead of baking soda or baking powder. Also known as salt of hartshorn, it used to be made from ground male deer's antlers, but is now chemically constructed. For these Swedish *Drömmar* it is worth getting hold of – once baked, it creates a chemical reaction which results in a melt-in-the-mouth, super-crispy but fragile finish.

120 g/1 stick butter

200 g/1 cup caster/granulated sugar

2 teaspoons vanilla sugar OR extract OR use the seeds from 1 vanilla pod/bean

80 ml/^{1}/$_3$ cup neutral-tasting oil (such as a good rapeseed or sunflower oil)

240 g/1^3/$_4$ cups plain/all-purpose flour

^{1}/$_2$ teaspoon baker's ammonia (otherwise known as ammonium carbonate/hartshorn/hjorthornssalt) available at speciality shops, online and in pharmacies.

^{1}/$_2$ teaspoon grated lemon zest

2 baking sheets, greased and lined with baking parchment

MAKES 30–35

Cream together the butter and caster/granulated sugar until pale and creamy using a stand mixer with a whisk attachment or a hand-held electric whisk. Next add the vanilla and oil and beat again until combined. Add the plain/all-purpose flour, baker's ammonia and lemon zest and mix briefly until you have an even dough.

Wrap the dough in clingfilm/plastic wrap and chill in the refrigerator for at least 30 minutes.

Preheat the oven to 150°C (300°F) Gas 2.

Roll the chilled dough into small balls of around 15 g/^{1}/$_2$ oz. each, trying not to overwork the dough. Evenly distribute the balls on the prepared baking sheets. There is no need to flatten the dough, as the biscuits/cookies will spread by themselves when baking.

Bake in the preheated oven for 20–25 minutes. The biscuits/cookies will not darken much in colour, so remove from the oven when they have only a slight tinge of gold and slightly cracked tops. Try not to open the oven door during at least the first half of the baking.

Leave to cool on a wire rack before storing in an airtight container. The baker's ammonia means the biscuits/cookies will stay crisp, even when baked at a low temperature.

Variations (omit the lemon zest):

For a hazelnut variation: add 50 g/^{1}/$_4$ cup finely chopped hazelnuts.

For an almond variation: add one whole almond on top before baking.

For a festive variation: add a pinch of ground saffron when you cream together the butter and sugar.

Note: When the biscuits bake, a strong smell of ammonia will be present – but don't worry, this is normal and the smell goes as soon as the biscuits cool. Just open the window a bit – and don't eat the dough before baking.

On a crisp, clear morning, you can savour the astonishingly beautiful Nordic autumn in all it's glory.

TRAYBAKES & NO BAKES

Sometimes you just need to be able to whip up a big tray of something – for the school bake sale, the cake day at the office or if you, like me, happen to always be running short of time and wondering where the day went. In this chapter are recipes for when you need to bake something that isn't too much of a fuss, but still delivers in taste and comfort.

Brunsviger

BRUNSWICK BUN

Fyn is an island in the middle of Denmark. A place of beautiful scenery, rich culture (the home of Hans Christian Andersen) and – the *Brunsviger* – a bread-like cake topped with lashings of brown sugar and butter. Think of a decadent cinnamon bun, baked open and sliced.

25 g/1 oz. fresh yeast or 13 g/2$^{1}/_{2}$ teaspoons dried/active dry yeast

250 ml/1 cup plus 1 tablespoon whole milk heated to 36°–37°C/97°–98°F

40 g/3$^{1}/_{4}$ tablespoons caster/granulated sugar

1 teaspoon ground cardamom

100 g/7 tablespoons very soft butter

1 egg yolk

1 teaspoon fine salt

350 g/2$^{1}/_{2}$ cups white strong/bread flour (approx.)

TOPPING:

175 g/1$^{1}/_{2}$ sticks butter, softened

225 g/1 cup plus 25 g/2 tablespoons dark brown soft sugar

4 generous tablespoons golden/light corn syrup

1 tablespoon ground cinnamon

a dash of vanilla extract

a 35 x 25-cm/14 x 9$^{3}/_{4}$-inch baking pan (with sides), greased and lined with baking parchment

MAKES ABOUT 12 GENEROUS SLICES

If using fresh yeast, add the yeast and milk to a stand mixer with a dough hook attached. Mix until the yeast has dissolved. If using dried/active dry yeast, pour the milk into a bowl. Sprinkle over the yeast and whisk together. Cover with clingfilm/plastic wrap and leave in a warm place for about 15 minutes until frothy and bubbly. Pour into the stand mixer with a dough hook attached.

Add the caster/granulated sugar and ground cardamom and continue to whisk. Next add the very soft butter and egg yolk. Combine the salt with the flour and add to the mixture bit by bit, continuing to mix with the dough hook for 5–6 minutes until you have a smooth (but still sticky) dough. Hold back on the flour if the dough gets too firm – you can always add more later. Cover the bowl with clingfilm/plastic wrap and leave to rise for about 20–30 minutes or until doubled in size.

To make the topping, whisk the softened butter with 200 g/1 cup of the dark brown soft sugar, the golden/light corn syrup, cinnamon and vanilla extract until you have a very soft, spreadable mixture.

Tip out the dough onto a floured surface and knead it through (add more flour if needed, as you now need a mouldable dough). Roll the dough out to roughly the size of the baking pan. Transfer the dough to the prepared pan and gently stretch it towards the sides of the pan. Prod shallow holes all over the dough with your fingers. The better the holes, the more hiding places for the topping – the best bit.

Spread over the topping with a spatula (blast quickly in the microwave if it needs loosening up) so that every bit of dough is covered. Scatter over the remaining 25 g/2 tablespoons dark brown soft sugar. Cover with clingfilm/plastic wrap and leave to rise for another 20 minutes.

Preheat the oven to 200°C (400°F) Gas 6.

Remove the clingfilm/plastic wrap from the cake and bake in the preheated oven for around 20–25 minutes or until cooked through. The topping should be sticky and shiny. Baking times may vary a little, so do keep an eye on it. Remove from oven and leave to cool. Cut into squares and serve. This cake is best enjoyed the same day it is made.

Eplekake
NORWEGIAN APPLE CAKE

This is a Norwegian apple cake – although to be fair, in my house, it is known more as 'I have too many apples, and this is a great way to use lots in one go and be nice to my neighbours' cake. It is a cake of generous size that is super-easy to throw together, and just perfect for sharing. You can easily halve the recipe if you don't have a small army to feed. Enjoy a generous piece with a dollop of vanilla crème fraîche or pouring cream on the side.

4-5 medium Granny Smith or similar tart apples (depending on the size of the apples)

a small squeeze of lemon juice

1 vanilla pod/bean, seeds scraped

300 g/2³/₄ sticks butter

300 g/1¹/₂ cups caster/granulated sugar

6 eggs

300 g/2¹/₄ cups plain/all-purpose flour or cake flour

2¹/₂ teaspoons baking powder

¹/₂ teaspoon salt

100 ml/¹/₂ cup minus ¹/₂ tablespoon double/heavy cream

2 teaspoons ground cinnamon

25 g/2¹/₂ tablespoons light brown soft sugar

50 g/³/₄ cup flaked/slivered almonds or other chopped nuts, to decorate

a 35 x 25-cm/14 x 9³/₄-inch rectangular baking pan, greased and lined with baking parchment

SERVES 12-14

Preheat the oven to 180°C (350°F) Gas 4.

Peel and core the apples, then cut into thin slices. If the slices are too thick they won't cook properly, so aim for around 0.5-0.75 cm/ ¹/₄ -³/₈ inch thick. Toss the slices in a little lemon juice to prevent discolouration and set aside.

Combine the vanilla seeds, butter and caster/granulated sugar in a large mixing bowl. Cream together until fluffy using the paddle attachment on the stand mixer or a hand-held electric whisk. Add the eggs, one by one, and mix until fully incorporated, scraping down the sides of the bowl if needed.

Sift in the dry ingredients and fold until smooth. Add the double/heavy cream and fold again to incorporate. Pour the mixture into the prepared pan and level the top.

Put the cinnamon, light brown soft sugar and apples into a plastic bag and shake to coat the apples evenly. Arrange the apples in a pretty pattern on top of the cake batter (I do three strips lengthways), then scatter over the flaked/slivered almonds.

Bake in the middle of the preheated oven for around 30-35 minutes or until a skewer inserted into the centre comes out clean. Note that if you change portion size or tin size, baking times will vary.

Slice into portions and enjoy warm or cold. This cake keeps well for at least 2-3 days stored in an airtight container.

Råg och blåbärmueslibar

RYE AND BLUEBERRY FLAPJACK

Who doesn't love a gooey, oaty flapjack bar? This one has the nice little twist of rye flakes added to the mixture. The consistency is a little different from your normal flapjack – the rye gives a more wholesome feel to the end result. Rye also has a deep almost nutty flavour to it, which I love. Add whatever dried berries tickle your fancy if you want to vary it a bit: try cranberries, lingonberries or goji berries. You can also add nuts and seeds if you wish.

175 g/1½ sticks butter

2 tablespoons golden/light corn syrup

1 tablespoon maple syrup

50 g/¼ cup dark brown soft sugar

100 g/½ cup light brown soft sugar

½ teaspoon ground cinnamon

½ teaspoon vanilla sugar OR extract OR use the seeds from 1 vanilla pod/bean

100 g/1 cup jumbo oats

200 g/2 cups rye flakes

100 g/¾ cup dried blueberries

a 20 x 30-cm/8 x 11¾-inch rectangular baking pan, greased and lined with baking parchment

MAKES 12

Preheat the oven to 160°C (325°F) Gas 3.

Put the butter, golden/light corn syrup, maple syrup and dark and light brown sugars into a saucepan. Heat together gently until just melted. Mix in the ground cinnamon and vanilla. Add the jumbo oats and rye flakes and stir well. Add the blueberries and stir again to evenly combine.

Spoon the mixture into the prepared pan. Pack the mixture down quite firmly using the back of a wooden spoon and press into all the corners (this will ensure you get a flapjack bar, not crumbs).

Bake in the preheated oven for around 20 minutes or until golden. The longer you bake, the crispier the result, so if you like your flapjack extra-chewy, take it out a little earlier.

Mark where the slices will be on the hot flapjack using a knife, then leave to cool completely in the pan before turning out and cutting properly into slices.

The flapjacks will keep well for a week stored in an airtight container.

Feeling hygge

I come from the land of *hygge*. Growing up, every aspect of living was governed around this wonderful word: a feeling of inner warmth, of mentally existing in a space where time is not a factor, but the state of just being, appreciating and feeling is all-encompassing.

First of all, let's sort out the pronunciation: *hygge* doesn't rhyme with *jiggy*. The *'y'* is soft and in Danish, it's a vowel. The actual sound of 'hy' doesn't really exist in English, so the closest way to explain how to pronounce it is 'who'. Add this to a hard 'g' sound ('g' like in gas) followed by a soft 'uh', and you have who-guh: *hygge*.

The concept of *hygge* isn't a new one. The word as we know it today has been in use since the late 19th century. It dates back to the Norse word *hyggja*, which meant something along the lines of feeling satisfied. In Sweden they use the word *mys,* and in Norway *kos* emphasises a similar meaning. We also like adding the word *hygge* to different seasons and situations. Every food magazine in Denmark will have a section of *julehygge* at Christmas and then another for *Påskehygge* at Easter.

Whenever I try to explain *hygge* to people, I always start with the word 'hug'. When you hug someone, you have to relax and just let yourself go. The feeling of a genuinely good hug is close to *hygge* (just shorter), and it's possible that the two words are related.

Scandinavians have become great at creating spaces around us that cultivate this feeling of inner warmth and togetherness. This is why you often see *hygge* described alongside candlelight, log fires or people sporting questionable woolly socks. But it is not exactly the same as cosiness: you can have a cosy house, a cosy chair, a cosy blanket, but these are physical objects. These things help to create *hygge*, but *hygge* itself is more a state of mind and being. Often, people describe *hygge* as something that can only take place when it is dark outside. Perhaps this is because, as Nordics, we are in darkness for half the year and *hygge* is what helps to carry us through. But you can just as easily find *hygge* on a summer's day in the garden.

While *hygge* is usually a social experience, you can of course *hygge* alone. It is, however, wonderful to appreciate the simple things with people you love. Whether sharing a cup of tea with an old friend in the garden, baking a batch of cookies with your children, or eating waffles after a long day of being outside in the snow.

I'm not going to lecture you on how to *hygge* like a Scandinavian as if it's a new thing, because you already know how to do it. Remember that lovely evening, surrounded by friends at home, maybe with a glass of wine or cup of tea and baked goods on the table. There were candles, the rain was beating on the window outside. There was laughter, conversation and a feeling of comfort. You remember it so fondly because you were present in the moment together. There was no before or after that mattered. That was *hygge*.

Lokis chokoladekage
LOKI'S BROWNIE

A good chocolate brownie rarely fails to satisfy. At the café, we have lots of different bits and pieces left over that work with chocolate, so our Kitchen Angels often make this easy brownie base and add whatever good stuff they feel like – from chocolate bars to sweets and fruit or nuts. The name, Loki, comes from Norse mythology. Loki was a trickster god and also a shape-shifter. This brownie often shape-shifts at the café: it may not be quite what it was the last time you had it, hence the name. Experiment with adding your own treats to the mix.

200 g/7 oz. good-quality 70% dark/bittersweet chocolate

250 g/2¼ sticks unsalted butter

275 g/1½ cups minus 2 tablespoons caster/granulated sugar

3 eggs

75 g/½ cup plus 1 tablespoon plain/all-purpose flour

50 g/2 oz. good-quality cocoa powder (we use Fazer cacao)

a pinch of salt

1 teaspoon vanilla sugar OR extract OR use the seeds from 1 vanilla pod/bean

150 g/5 oz. filling of your choice – see end of method for suggestions

a 20 x 20-cm/8 x 8-inch square baking pan, greased and lined with baking parchment

MAKES 9–12

Preheat the oven to 170°C (340°F) Gas 4.

Melt the chocolate and butter in a heatproof bowl set over a pan of barely simmering water. Do not let the base of the bowl touch the water. Alternatively, you can melt the chocolate in the microwave, but take care to just melt, don't cook it. Set aside to cool.

Beat together the caster/granulated sugar and eggs by hand using a balloon whisk in a large mixing bowl. There is no need to beat in loads of air as you don't want the brownie to rise too much. Ensure the melted chocolate-butter has cooled sufficiently, then stir into the sugar-egg mixture.

Sift the plain/all-purpose flour, cocoa powder and salt into the bowl. Add the vanilla and fold with a spatula until smooth. Take care not to overwork the mixture. Fold in 100 g/3½ oz. of your chosen filling. Pour the mixture into the prepared pan and sprinkle the remaining filling on top.

Bake in the preheated oven for 25–30 minutes or until a skewer inserted into the side comes out clean – the middle can still be gooey but it should not wobble when you shake the pan. Leave to cool, then cut into squares to serve.

Filling suggestions: 150 g/5 oz. nuts such as walnut, pecan, macadamia or Brazil nuts. Your favourite sweets/candy: marshmallows, chopped Daim bars, toffees, liquorice, soft nougat praline chunks, mint chocolates or chocolate buttons. Dried fruit such as raisins or cherries.

Note: Baking times will vary. Brownies are quite forgiving if you cook them on lower heat for a longer time – so keep checking the edges and just make sure you don't overbake. It's better to slightly underbake a brownie, if anything, so take it out a bit earlier rather than give it that extra few minutes.

Hvid chokoladekage med lavendel og citron

BLONDIE WITH LAVENDER AND LEMON

This is a super-simple yet amazing version of a blondie – quick to stir together and bake. It's fair to say that a lot of traditional Nordic recipes use the same spices and flavours again and again, because these are our baking heritage. Sometimes, well, a little change is needed. I love using lavender in baking – but I do it with care. Nobody wants their cake to taste of grandma's cupboards. The lemon in this blondie pairs well with the lavender, ensuring it's not overpowering but, as with everything, you can vary the amounts to suit your taste.

150 g/1¼ sticks unsalted butter

225 g/1¾ cups plain/all-purpose flour

1 teaspoon baking powder

½ teaspoon salt

2 tablespoons lavender sugar (see note)

200 g/1 cup caster/granulated sugar

2 eggs plus 1 yolk

grated zest of 1 lemon

200 g/7 oz. white chocolate, chopped

50 g/¼ cup macadamia nuts, roughly chopped (optional)

icing/confectioners' sugar, for dusting

a 20 x 20-cm/8 x 8-inch square baking pan, greased and lined with baking parchment

MAKES 9–12

Preheat the oven to 200°C (400°F) Gas 6.

Melt the butter and set aside to cool a little.

Sift the plain/all-purpose flour, baking powder and salt into a bowl. Stir in the lavender sugar.

In a separate large mixing bowl, stir together the caster/granulated sugar and melted butter. Next add the eggs and lemon zest and stir again until smooth. Fold in the flour, then the chopped white chocolate and macadamia nuts, if using. The mixture should be quite thick.

Pour the mixture into the prepared baking pan and level the surface. Bake in the preheated oven for around 20 minutes or until cooked but still slightly squidgy in the middle. Take care not to overbake.

Remove from oven and turn out almost immediately to cool on a wire rack. Dust with icing/confectioners' sugar and garnish with additional lavender or chopped nuts if desired. Cut into squares to serve.

Note: For the lavender sugar, I use equal parts food-grade lavender to sugar and pulse it until fine in a spice grinder or food processor, sifting out any large pieces that remain.

Silviakaka
SILVIA CAKE

I have tried my best to find origins and meanings for the cakes in this book. Sometimes it is not easy, as things get a little lost in history. This cake is known as Silvia cake in Sweden, presumably after the Queen. My friend Hannah got her Swedish grandmother on the case, who found out the base is an old version of sponge cake (*sockerkaka*) with added water known as *fattigmanskaka* – or poor man's cake. The topping was later added. Why water is added other than to thin the batter I'm not sure, but it doesn't work well without it. Be careful when you make this – it is quite easy to just have a nibble and then everything goes downhill from there and you won't have enough for your *fredagshygge* (Friday cosy time).

3 eggs plus one yolk

160 g/³/4 cup minus 1 tablespoon caster/granulated sugar

80 g/¹/2 cup minus 1 tablespoon light brown soft sugar

seeds from ¹/2 vanilla pod/bean

200 g/1¹/2 cups plain/all-purpose flour or cake flour

2 teaspoons baking powder

a pinch of salt

ICING/FROSTING:

150 g/1¹/4 sticks butter

150 g/³/4 cup caster/granulated sugar

seeds from the ¹/2 of the vanilla pod/bean

2 egg yolks

a few drops of lemon juice

75 g/1 cup desiccated/dried shredded coconut

a 20 x 20-cm/8 x 8-inch square baking pan, greased and lined with baking parchment

SERVES 12–16

Preheat the oven to 180°C (350°F) Gas 4.

In a stand mixer with the whisk attachment (or using a hand-held electric whisk), beat the eggs with the caster/granulated sugar, light brown soft sugar and vanilla seeds until thick, light and fluffy.

Sift together the flour, baking powder and salt, then fold into the beaten sugar and egg mixture. Slowly add 100 ml/¹/3 cup cold water and fold until incorporated.

Bake in the middle of the preheated oven for around 25–30 minutes or until well-risen, golden brown and springy to the touch. A skewer inserted into the centre should come out clean.

Make the icing/frosting as soon as the cake is out of the oven. Melt the butter gently in a saucepan, taking care not to brown it. Add the sugar and vanilla and allow to dissolve. Add the egg yolks and whisk until smooth over a low heat. Remove from the heat and add 50 g/¹/4 cup of the desiccated/dried shredded coconut and stir to a thick icing/frosting.

Preheat the grill/broiler. Spread the icing/frosting over the cake, then place it under a hot grill/broiler for a minute or so until lightly caramelized. Remove from grill/broiler and sprinkle over enough coconut to cover the top. Allow to cool before cutting into squares to serve.

Note: thank you to Therese for reminding me of this cake – we have since added it to our range at the café, as it is such a perfect fika cake!

Romkugler
RUM TREATS

A true 'waste not want not' treat. Every Danish bakery has loads of cakes that are, like these *romkugler* or rum balls, basically made from leftover pastries. It makes a lot of sense for bakers to find ways to use their leftovers in really delicious ways. It is best to avoid using leftovers containing raisins or strong flavours, as these will come through in the end result. I usually use a cinnamon swirl or two, some sponge cake and maybe some chocolate cake or a muffin. I do have the advantage of always having plenty of leftover pastries around, but you can freeze bits and just defrost and make this when you have enough.

500 g/1lb. leftover Danish pastries and/or cake – ideally mixture of both

2–3 tablespoons good quality raspberry jam/jelly

100 g/³/₄ cup icing/confectioners' sugar (add less if your cakes are a really sweet variety)

100 g/7 tablespoons softened butter

2 tablespoons cocoa powder

vanilla essence

2–3 teaspoons rum extract or essence (I use quite a concentrated one – you may need to add a bit more, as you want it to have a good punchy flavour)

a handful of oats (optional)

dark/bittersweet or milk/semisweet chocolate vermicelli strands, to decorate

MAKES 10–15

Roughly tear any Danish pastries into bite-sized pieces and crumble up any cakes you are using. In a stand mixer using the paddle attachment or in a food processor, blend the shredded and crumbled pastries and cakes with the rest of the ingredients (apart from the oats and the chocolate vermicelli) until evenly mixed. Alternatively, you can do this by hand with a wooden spoon in a mixing bowl, but it will take longer.

Taste the mixture – it may need more cocoa powder, rum extract or even icing/confectioners' sugar. Because this is made with leftovers, the taste will vary a bit. If you feel it needs more texture you can add a handful of oats.

Chill the mixture in the refrigerator for about an hour to firm up.

Roll into balls a bit larger than the size of a golf ball and roll in the chocolate vermicelli strands to evenly coat. Chill again in the refrigerator until you are ready to serve.

Rum treats will keep well for 2–3 days wrapped in clingfilm/plastic wrap and stored in the refrigerator.

In the snowy forests we all cosy
up inside with candles and log fires.

EVERYDAY FIKA

Meeting up for coffee and something sweet is one of the most popular Scandinavian pastimes, and we do it several times a day. It allows us to sit down and connect with the people around us, to take a bit of time out and just have a good old chit-chat. Our love of *fika* means we have a huge array of tasty, staple no-fuss cakes that are not hard to make, but fit perfectly on the kitchen table, ready to slice and share.

Blåbärsmuffins
BLUEBERRY STUDMUFFINS

At the café, people were always asking for a breakfast option that wasn't too 'green' but also not overly sweet. Our wholesome studmuffins are somewhere between a healthy muffin and those sugary ones you find at many coffee shops.

250 g/2$\frac{1}{2}$ cups spelt flour

100 g/$\frac{1}{2}$ cup light brown soft sugar

75 g/1 cup rolled/old-fashioned porridge oats, plus extra for topping

$\frac{1}{2}$ teaspoon salt

1 teaspoon bicarbonate of/baking soda

2 teaspoons baking powder

1 teaspoon vanilla sugar OR extract OR use the seeds from 1 vanilla pod/bean

1$\frac{1}{2}$ teaspoons ground cinnamon

$\frac{1}{2}$ teaspoon grated nutmeg

2 eggs

200 ml/$\frac{3}{4}$ cup whole milk

75 ml/$\frac{1}{3}$ cup sunflower oil

2 teaspoons apple sauce or compote

2 teaspoons maple syrup

2 ripe bananas

100 g/$\frac{3}{4}$ cup frozen or fresh blueberries

a muffin tray lined with large tulip muffin cases, or regular muffin cases

MAKES 6–7 LARGE OR 10–12 SMALL

Preheat the oven to 180°C (350°F) Gas 4.

Combine all the dry ingredients in a mixing bowl and stir together.

Mix all the wet ingredients together in another large bowl (apart from the bananas and berries). Add the wet ingredients to the dry ingredients and mix using a wooden spoon until just combined.

Roughly mash the banana and add to the mixture. If using frozen blueberries, fold these in now. Portion out the batter into the muffin cases. If using fresh blueberries, add these to the batter now. Top each muffin with a scattering of porridge oats.

Bake in the preheated oven for about 30 minutes or until a skewer inserted into the middle comes out clean. The baking time will vary depending on the size of the muffins. Cool on a wire rack.

Saffran och päronkaka
SAFFRON BUNDT CAKE WITH PEARS

Across Scandinavia in December you will likely be offered a saffron-flavoured Lucia bun in honour of the Feast of St Lucia. I also make this beautiful, light saffron cake with pears.

30 g/¼ cup breadcrumbs
50 g/3½ tablespoons butter
100 ml/⅓ cup plus 1 tablespoon whole milk
0.5 g/½ teaspoon ground saffron
2 large or 3 small pears
a little lemon juice
325 g/1½ cups plus 2 tablespoons caster/granulated sugar
4 eggs
300 g/2¼ cups plain/all-purpose flour
2 teaspoons baking powder
1 teaspoon vanilla extract
½ teaspoon of salt
50 g/¼ cup Greek yogurt
icing/confectioners' sugar, for dusting

a 25-cm/9-inch Bundt pan or ring pan, greased

SERVES 10

Preheat the oven to 180°C (350°F) Gas 4.

Dust the greased Bundt or ring pan with the breadcrumbs, tipping out the excess.

Melt the butter and add the milk and ground saffron. Stir to combine and set aside to infuse.

Peel and core the pears and cut into bite-sized chunks. Add a dash of lemon juice, stir and set aside.

In a mixing bowl, beat the sugar and eggs until thick, light and fluffy using a balloon whisk or a hand-held electric whisk. Mix the remaining dry ingredients together and sift into the egg mixture. Fold in until incorporated. Add the Greek yogurt and saffron-milk mixture and fold gently until completely combined. Pour the cake batter into the prepared Bundt pan. Add the pieces of pear – these will sink down during baking.

Bake for around 30–35 minutes in the preheated oven or until a skewer inserted into the middle comes out clean. Leave to cool in the pan before turning out onto a serving tray. Dust with icing/confectioners' sugar and serve, sliced, with a good dollop of whipped cream.

Mjuk pepperkaka
GINGERBREAD CAKE WITH LINGONBERRIES

This cake is for those days when the wind is blowing outside, the rain smashes against the window and nobody has any intention of leaving the house. I think most Scandinavians love autumn and winter, despite the cold and dark, but I admit that perhaps I love it more than most. The childhood longing for snow and Christmas never left me as I got older and I can think of nothing nicer than spending time with the people I love, at home – ultimate *hygge*. If you can't find lingonberries, raspberries or other tart berries also work well with this cake.

175 g/1¹/₂ sticks butter

3 eggs

150 g/³/₄ cup caster/granulated sugar

100 g/¹/₂ cup light brown soft sugar

300 g/2¹/₄ cups plain/all-purpose flour or cake flour

2 teaspoons baking powder

2 teaspoons ground cinnamon

1 teaspoon ground ginger

1 teaspoon ground cloves

¹/₂ teaspoon vanilla extract

¹/₂ teaspoon ground cardamom

a pinch of salt

220 ml/1 cup whole milk

ICING/FROSTING:

175 g/1¹/₂ sticks butter, softened

180 g/1 cup cream cheese

400 g/3 cups icing/confectioners' sugar

50 g/ ¹/₄ cup lingonberries, defrosted (plus extra for decorating)

freshly squeezed juice of ¹/₂ lime

3 x 18-cm/7-inch round cake pans, greased and lined with baking parchment

SERVES 8–12

Preheat the oven to 180°C (350°F) Gas 4.

Melt the butter and set aside to cool a little.

Using a balloon whisk or a hand-held electric whisk, beat the eggs with the caster/granulated and light brown soft sugar until light and fluffy.

Combine the dry ingredients in a separate bowl, then sift into the egg mixture and fold in gently. Add the melted, cooled butter and whole milk and fold again until incorporated.

Divide the mixture between the three prepared cake pans and bake in the preheated oven for around 15 minutes or until well-risen, golden brown and springy to the touch. A skewer inserted into the middle should come out clean. Turn the cakes out onto a wire rack to cool.

To make the icing/frosting, combine the butter, cream cheese and icing/confectioners' sugar and beat on high speed using a stand mixer or a hand-held electric whisk until smooth. Drain the excess juice from the defrosted lingonberries, reserving a little, then add to the mixture. Beat again until light and fluffy. Add a few drops of the reserved juice at the end to give a pale pink colour to the icing/frosting.

To assemble the cake, place a sponge layer on your serving dish and spread over a layer of icing/frosting. Repeat the process with the second and third layers, reserving a generous layer of icing/frosting for the final layer. Scatter with more lingonberries to decorate.

Tip: If you don't have three equal-sized pans you can bake this as one cake and then cut into three layers. Adjust the baking time to suit.

Vores banankage
THAT BANANA CAKE

We've been making this banana cake since ScandiKitchen first opened. We wanted to make one that wasn't like all the others: this one is lighter in colour and feels really indulgent with the sweet, tangy frosting. You can use either *filmjölk* (a kind of Swedish soured milk) or yogurt in this cake, but the soured milk gives a slightly lighter finish. Both are delicious.

3 ripe bananas
1 teaspoon lemon juice
125 g/1¹/8 sticks butter, softened
300 g/1¹/2 cups caster/granulated sugar
3 eggs
200 g/1¹/2 cups plain/all-purpose flour or cake flour
50 g/¹/2 cup cornflour/cornstarch
¹/2 teaspoon salt
1¹/2 teaspoons baking powder
2 teaspoons vanilla sugar OR extract OR use the seeds from 1 vanilla pod/bean
250 g/8 oz. Greek yogurt, OR natural yogurt OR 250ml/1 cup filmjölk

ICING/FROSTING:
125 g/1¹/8 sticks butter, softened
125 g/¹/2 cup cream cheese
1 teaspoon vanilla sugar OR extract OR use the seeds from 1 vanilla pod/bean
freshly squeezed juice of ¹/2 lime
300 g/2¹/2 cups icing/confectioners' sugar, sifted
chopped pecan nuts, to decorate

a 23-cm/9-inch springform/springclip round cake pan, greased and lined with baking parchment

SERVES 8–10

Preheat the oven to 180°C (350°F) Gas 4.

Blend the bananas with the lemon juice in a food processor to a purée and set aside.

Cream together the butter and sugar in a stand mixer (or using a hand-held electric whisk) until very smooth, light and fluffy. Add the eggs, one at a time, beating well with each addition.

Sift the dry ingredients together in a separate bowl and then fold into the batter. Add the banana purée, bit by bit, and fold in. Then gently fold in the yogurt or soured milk until combined.

Pour the batter into the prepared cake pan and bake in the preheated oven for around 50–55 minutes or until golden brown and springy to the touch. A skewer inserted into the middle should come out clean. The baking time with this cake varies depending on the size of the bananas that have gone in, so keep checking.

Turn out the cake and leave to cool on a wire rack. It must be completely cool before adding the topping, so ideally make it several hours in advance.

For the icing/frosting, whisk together the butter, cream cheese, vanilla, lime juice and icing/confectioners' sugar for several minutes until very smooth and creamy. If it becomes too soft then chill in the refrigerator for 20 minutes before use.

Spread the icing/frosting generously onto the cooled cake and decorate with a small handful of chopped pecan nuts.

Rabarber og crème kage

RHUBARB AND CUSTARD CAKE

Every year when the rhubarb season starts, we make this cake. The custard isn't really 'custard' but a baked pastry cream. Luckily for us, we always have loads of rhubarb at the café. This is because one of our regulars at the café, John, has an allotment nearby where the rhubarb seems to grow faster than he can eat it. We exchange huge amounts of his delicious rhubarb for coffee - and everybody wins. It's one of my favourite local trade agreements!

150–200 g/5–7 oz./^{3}/$_4$–1 cup Pastry Cream (see page 14)

175 g/1^1/$_2$ sticks butter

200 g/1 cup caster/granulated sugar

4 eggs, lightly beaten

200 g/1^1/$_2$ cups plain/all-purpose flour or cake flour

1 teaspoon vanilla sugar OR extract OR use the seeds from 1 vanilla pod/bean

^{1}/$_2$ teaspoon salt

1^1/$_2$ teaspoons baking powder

TOPPING:

400 g/14 oz. rhubarb

30 g/^{1}/$_4$ stick butter

50 g/^{1}/$_4$ cup caster/granulated sugar

2 teaspoons ground cardamom

a 23-cm/9-inch springform/springclip round cake pan, greased and lined with baking parchment

SERVES 8

Preheat the oven to 180°C (350°F) Gas 4.

First, make the topping. Wash the rhubarb and chop into 2 cm/^{3}/$_4$ inch pieces. In a saucepan set over low heat, melt the butter then stir in the caster/granulated sugar and ground cardamom. Add the chopped rhubarb, stir to coat in the butter and stew for 2–3 minutes to start the cooking process, then remove from the heat and set aside to infuse.

To make the cake, cream together the butter and sugar in a stand mixer with a whisk attachment (or using a hand-held electric whisk) until pale and fluffy. Add the eggs to the mixture bit by bit, whisking constantly but stopping to scrape down the sides of the bowl if necessary. Ensure all the egg is fully incorporated before adding more.

Combine the dry ingredients and sift into the egg mixture. Fold in until incorporated. Pour the batter into the prepared cake pan and spread out evenly. Spread the pastry cream evenly on top of the batter.

Remove the rhubarb from the syrup and scatter over the cake. Reserve the syrup for drizzling over the cake once it's cooked.

Bake for about 60 minutes in the preheated oven (lowering the heat if the top gets too dark). A skewer inserted into the middle of the cake should come out clean, however the pastry cream will remain a bit wet. Remove from oven and allow to cool slightly before drizzling with leftover rhubarb syrup and cutting into slices to serve.

Honningkage
HONEY CAKE

Deliciously moist honey cakes became popular in Denmark in the late 1700s, with a strong influence from the German *Lebkuchen*. Omit the raw yolk from the buttercream if you prefer.

125 ml/$^1/_2$ cup runny honey

80 ml/$^1/_3$ cup dark syrup (or golden/light corn syrup)

50 g/$^1/_4$ cup caster/granulated sugar

2 eggs plus 2 egg yolks

300 g/2$^1/_4$ cups plain /all-purpose flour or cake flour

1$^1/_2$ teaspoons bicarbonate of/baking soda

2 teaspoons ground cinnamon

$^1/_2$ teaspoon ground cardamom

1 teaspoon ground ginger

1 teaspoon ground cloves

a pinch of salt

grated zest from one orange

280 ml/1$^1/_4$ cups buttermilk

150 ml/$^2/_3$ cup double/heavy cream

BUTTERCREAM FILLING:

100 g/$^1/_2$ cup caster/granulated sugar

125 g/ 1$^1/_8$ sticks butter, softened

1 egg yolk (optional)

1 teaspoon vanilla sugar OR extract OR use the seeds from $^1/_2$ vanilla pod/bean

CHOCOLATE TOPPING:

30 g/$^1/_4$ cup cocoa powder

80 g/$^2/_3$ cup sifted icing/confectioners' sugar

a few spoons hot water

sprinkles, to decorate

a rectangular 35 x 25-cm/ 14 x 9 $^3/_4$-inch cake pan, greased and lined with baking parchment

Preheat the oven to 160°C (325°F) Gas 3.

Combine the honey, syrup and caster/granulated sugar with 100 ml/ $^1/_3$ cup water in a saucepan over a low heat until melted together. Leave to cool until tepid.

Crack the eggs into a stand mixer (or mixing bowl and use a hand-held electric whisk) and beat to combine. Slowly add the tepid syrup mixture into the eggs, beating continuously on high speed.

Sift all the dry ingredients together, then fold into the egg and sugar mixture until smooth. Add the orange zest, buttermilk and double/heavy cream and fold again until smooth.

Pour the batter into the prepared cake pan and bake for around 20 minutes or until well-risen, golden brown and springy to the touch. A skewer inserted into the middle should come out clean. Leave to cool for a few minutes in the pan, then turn out onto a wire rack and allow to cool completely before filling.

To make the buttercream filling, gently heat 30 ml/$^1/_8$ cup water with the caster/granulated sugar in a pan until dissolved to make a sugar syrup. Leave to cool.

Beat the butter, egg yolk (if using) and vanilla together on high speed and slowly add the sugar syrup, bit by bit, whisking well with each addition. Continue beating for several minutes until creamy and fluffy.

To assemble the cake, cut the sides off the sponge cake to make a neat rectangle. Cut the cake down the middle lengthways and place one piece on a serving tray. Add enough buttercream to cover generously, then place the other half on top.

To make the chocolate topping, place the cocoa powder and icing/confectioners' sugar in a bowl. Gradually add tablespoons of hot water, bit by bit, and keep stirring until you get a smooth, sticky and glossy consistency. Add more sugar if it gets too runny, or more water if too dry. Spread neatly on top of the cake using a palette knife and decorate with sprinkles. Slice into squares to serve.

MAKES 12–14

How to fika

If you know any Swedish people or have been to Sweden, you are likely to have encountered the word *fika*. Swedes love the word and use it both when they speak Swedish and other languages, as it is hard to find another word that conveys exactly the same thing: to meet up for a chat over a drink and a bite of something to eat, usually baked.

The word *fika* is both a noun and a verb. The name of the action of 'taking a *fika*' and the name of the delicious baked treats themselves.

The word 'coffee break' would be the closest translation in English, but this doesn't always include the social element of a *fika*. Whether you *fika* at a café, at work, at someone's house or just at home, the vital element is that it is done with other people, because engaging in conversation is essential.

Fika is a very casual concept – Scandinavians usually *fika* with colleagues twice a day in a *fika* room (most workplaces have these), over a cup of tea or coffee and a bite of something sweet.

The length of a *fika* break varies – if you're at work, it might be 10–15 minutes, but if you are in town with friends, it can be several hours. There are also different kinds of *fika* depending on the occasion. An evening *fika* with your family is called *kvällsfika* and may involve savoury food, as well as cake. You can even arrange to have a *fika* date, which is just like a normal date except casual – you don't need to invest in a new dress.

It is often implied that you need to drink coffee in order to *fika*, but actually, any non-alcoholic drink is fine. Scandinavians drink more strong coffee than anyone else in the world, so this is perhaps why *fika* is synonymous with coffee.

The cinnamon bun is one of the most popular choices of baked goods for a *fika* – I often say that the smell of a batch of freshly baked buns can stop anyone from remembering what they are supposed to be doing – but any of the baked goods in this book are perfectly suitable, whether biscuits, buns or a slice of fancy cake.

There is debate on the origin of the word *fika*, which first became popular in the 1960s – although Swedes have most certainly *fika'ed* for centuries. One theory is that it simply comes from the French slang word for café, *feka*. Another theory is that it comes from a dialect word for coffee from the Dalarna region (*fäka* or *fik*), first mentioned in a book in 1733. Another possibility is the old Stockholm term for meeting for coffee – *fikhäck*. Yet another theory is that *fika* comes from the Swedish military, where cups had the word *fic* on them. In 2009, Professor Lars-Gunnar Andersson from the

University of Gothenburg theorized that it evolved from the word *kaffe* (or *kaffi*) without much historic meaning at all. Wherever it comes from, *fika* is as much part of Swedish culture as ABBA, meatballs and red Dala horses.

In recent years, the concept of *fika* has become more and more popular outside Sweden, as the coffee revolution has taken hold across the world and we all try to take time out of our busy lives to enjoy the company of others. Since we opened ScandiKitchen, we have seen a huge increase in people choosing to sit down mid-morning for a cinnamon bun and a coffee, and again later on in the afternoon with a slice of cake, sometimes combining this little *fika* with a casual meeting with colleagues. Fewer people now take coffee to drink on the go. Are we turning a corner and going back to connecting with each other instead of always being in a hurry? I certainly hope so.

Kladdkaka
STICKY WHITE CHOCOLATE CAKE

Every café in Sweden has a *kladdkaka* or 'sticky cake' on the counter and they outsell the other cakes two to one. It is the same at our place: there is just something about a slightly underbaked, chocolatey mess that just is so intensely alluring. Getting the right baking time may take a few attempts – but the general rule is: if you think it needs a few minutes more, take it out now. Here is a recipe that you can make with your preferred chocolate.

150 g/1¼ sticks butter

150 g/5 oz. good-quality white chocolate (or milk/semisweet or dark/bittersweet chocolate) broken into pieces

2 eggs

200 g/1 cup caster/granulated sugar

150 g/1 cup plain/all-purpose flour or cake flour

a pinch of salt

2 teaspoons vanilla sugar OR extract OR use the seeds from 1 vanila pod/bean

½ teaspoon grated lemon zest

optional toppings (see method)

a 23-cm/9-inch springform/springclip round cake pan, greased and lined with baking parchment

Note: For the milk/semisweet chocolate kladdkaka, omit the lemon zest and instead add 2 tablespoons golden/light corn syrup and extend cooking time slightly

SERVES 6–8

Preheat the oven to 180°C (350°F) Gas 4.

Melt the butter in a saucepan over low heat. Remove from the heat and stir in the white chocolate pieces until melted. Set aside.

Beat together the eggs and caster/granulated sugar until pale and fluffy in a stand mixer or using a hand-held electric whisk. Sift the dry ingredients into a separate bowl and fold gently into the egg and sugar mixture. Fold in the lemon zest and chocolate-butter until combined.

Pour into the prepared cake pan and place in the preheated oven immediately. Bake for about 15–17 minutes until the cake is just under-baked. The middle should still be really sticky and only the side should be fully baked. Keep an eye on it, as baking times will vary. If it wobbles, it still needs a little more time in the oven. A skewer inserted 2 cm/¾ inch from the edge should come out clean.

Leave the cake to cool in the pan for at least an hour before transferring to a serving plate. If you think you have overbaked it, then remove from tin immediately to stop baking process. Serve the kladdkaka on its own or with one of the toppings below:

Raspberry coulis: Mash 120 g/1 cup raspberries and place in a saucepan with 2 tablespoons icing/confectioners' sugar. Heat and boil for a few minutes, then strain through a sieve. This topping works well with the white chocolate *kladdkaka*.

Double chocolate: Finely chop 50 g/2 oz. of your favourite chocolate and mix with whipped cream and ½ teaspoon cocoa powder. Works with milk/semisweet or dark/bittersweet chocolate *kladdkaka*.

Fresh mixed berries: Top with fresh redcurrants and blueberries and dust with icing/confectioners' sugar just before serving with whipped cream. This topping works well with all types of chocolate *kladdkaka*.

Hjortronkaka med vit chocklad
CLOUDBERRY AND WHITE CHOCOLATE CAKE

The thing with cloudberries is, they are evasive little things. Not only are they near impossible to cultivate, they have a short season and grow in such a way that every time you try and pick them, most burst in your hand. Their flavour is unlike any other berry – tart yet sweet but very subtle when cooked. For me, they are my favourite berry. This is one of those cakes you can whip up in a jiffy and I have used cloudberry jam here, which is the only form most people who don't live near the Arctic Circle get to taste. Serve with fresh cloudberries if you can find them, or whipped cream mixed with extra cloudberry jam/jelly.

175 g/1¹/₂ sticks butter, softened

200 g/1 cup caster/granulated sugar

4 eggs

220g /1²/₃ cups plain/all-purpose flour or cake flour

a pinch of salt

1 teaspoon vanilla sugar OR extract OR use the seeds from 1 vanilla pod/bean

2 teaspoons baking powder

100 g/³/₄ cup white chocolate, chopped

150 ml/¹/₂ cup cloudberry jam/jelly

100 ml/¹/₃ cup buttermilk or natural yogurt

1–2 teaspooons freshly squeezed lemon juice

melted white chocolate, to decorate

extra cloudberries, to decorate (optional)

TO SERVE:

250 ml/1 cup plus 1 tablespoon whipping cream

a dash of vanilla extract

extra jam/jelly

a 1.4-litre/6-cup Bundt cake pan/mould or ring pan, greased

SERVES 10

Preheat the oven to 180°C (350°F) Gas 4.

Cream together the butter and sugar until fluffy in a stand mixer or using a hand-held electric whisk. Add the eggs one at a time, beating well to make sure each is fully incorporated. Scrape down the sides of the bowl if needed.

In a separate bowl, combine all the dry ingredients (apart from the chocolate). Sift into the butter mixture and fold until combined. Next add the chopped white chocolate, jam/jelly, buttermilk or yogurt and lemon juice and fold again.

Pour the cake batter into the prepared pan and bake for around 30 minutes or until well-risen and springy to the touch. A skewer inserted into the middle should come out clean. Leave to cool before turning out onto a serving plate.

Add extra berries and drizzle with melted white chocolate to decorate.

Whip the cream to soft peaks with the vanilla extract; fold in the jam/jelly, to taste and serve alongside the cake.

Mazarintårta med plommon och peppar

MAZARIN TART WITH PLUMS AND BLACK PEPPER

We Scandinavians love mazarin – it's our version of a frangipane, made using actual marzipan. We also tend to add plain/all-purpose flour to the mixture when we bake it, which results in a lovely cakey finish, one that complements most fruits and berries. Towards October when there isn't much going on fruit-wise, plums are a good option for baking and prove a welcome break from overdosing on apples. The black pepper gives this tart a nice kick.

7–8 ripe plums

2 tablespoons caster/granulated sugar

1 vanilla pod/bean

freshly ground black pepper

1/2 batch Sweet Shortcrust Pastry Dough (see page 14)

MAZARIN:

150 g/5 oz. store-bought marzipan (or see page 15 for basic recipe), cubed

100 g/1/2 cup caster/granulated sugar

100 g/7 tablespoons butter, softened

2 eggs

50 g/heaped 1/3 cup plain/all-purpose flour

a pinch of salt

icing/confectioners' sugar, for dusting

crème fraîche or sour cream, to serve (optional)

a 25-cm/9-inch loose-based flan/tart pan

SERVES 8–10

Preheat the oven to 180°C (350°F) Gas 4.

First, prepare the fruit. Remove the stones/pits from the plums, cut the fruit into thick slices and set aside.

Put the caster/granulated sugar into a bowl. Slice open the vanilla pod/bean and remove the seeds with a sharp knife. Add these to the sugar. Grind the mixture with the back of a spoon to lightly crush the seeds and mix the sugar with the vanilla. Next add a good few grinds of black pepper (about 7–8 or to taste). Add the plums to the bowl and mix together gently so that the fruit is coated in the sugar.

Lightly flour a work surface and roll out the sweet shortcrust pastry. Line the flan/tart pan as neatly as you can with the pastry.

To make the mazarin, mix the together the marzipan and caster/granulated sugar until combined, using a stand mixer with the paddle attachment or a wooden spoon, then add the softened butter. Mix again until smooth then add the eggs, one by one, ensuring they are well incorporated. Sift in the flour and salt and fold into the mixture.

Spoon out the mazarin onto the pastry base and spread out evenly. Shake the fruit again to ensure all the slices are covered with the vanilla, sugar and pepper mixture. Arrange the plums in a pretty pattern on top of the mazarin.

Add a little more black pepper on top and bake in the preheated oven for around 45–50 minutes or until the pastry is nicely browned at the edges and the mazarin has set.

Remove from the oven and allow to cool slightly. Dust with icing/confectioners' sugar and serve slices with whipped crème fraîche or sour cream on the side.

Citronmåne
LEMON MOON CAKE

Around 45 years ago, a big Danish cake producer started making a cake called *citronmåne* or lemon moon, owing to the crescent shape and yellow colour. It quickly became one of those popular, convenient cakes your mum would pick up at the store when she didn't have time to bake and the neighbour was due to pop over to discuss the latest gossip. This tangy, beautiful version of the supermarket classic is several degrees more delicious than the plastic-wrapped variety. It has certainly earned its prominent place in our 'staples' recipe book at the café.

200 g/1¾ sticks butter

200 g/1 cup caster/granulated sugar

100 g/3½ oz. store-bought marzipan (or see page 15 for basic recipe)

seeds from 1 vanilla pod/bean

5 eggs plus 1 yolk

200 g/1½ cups plain/all-purpose flour or cake flour

1 teaspoon baking powder

a pinch of salt

grated zest and freshly squeezed juice of 1 lemon

ICING/FROSTING:

150 g/1¼ cups icing/confectioners' sugar, sifted

freshly squeezed lemon juice (to taste)

1 tablespoon hot water

grated zest of ½ lemon

1 teaspoon vanilla sugar OR extract OR use the seeds from 1 vanilla pod/bean

chopped almonds, to decorate

a round 22-cm/8-inch diameter springform/springclip pan, greased and lined with baking parchment

SERVES 8

Preheat the oven to 160°C (300°F) Gas 2.

In a stand mixer or using a hand-held electric whisk, cream together the butter and sugar until pale and fluffy. Grate the marzipan into the mixture, add the seeds from the vanilla pod/bean and mix again. Next add the eggs, one at a time, ensuring you incorporate fully between each addition and scraping down the sides of the bowl if necessary.

Combine the flour, baking powder and salt. Sift into the cake mixture and fold with a spatula until combined. Add the lemon zest and half the juice and fold again. If the mixture seems too thick, you can add a bit more lemon juice.

Pour the mixture into the prepared pan and bake in the preheated oven for around 1 hour or until a skewer inserted into the middle comes out clean. Turn out the cake onto a wire rack and leave to cool completely before decorating.

To make the icing/frosting, place the icing/confectioners' in a bowl and add 2 tablespoons lemon juice and 1 tablespoon hot water, mixing in well. Add more lemon juice until you get to the consistency of runny honey: spreadable, but not so liquid that it runs off the cake. Add the lemon zest and vanilla and stir until smooth. If the icing/frosting becomes too runny, add a bit more icing/confectioners' sugar.

Decorate with chopped almonds if you wish, or make a pattern with a darker coloured icing for a more traditional look.

Suksesskake
SUCCESS CAKE

Ah, how I love the names of cakes from Norway. *Suksess* means success, so this cake really does talk itself up a bit and sets expectations high! It does not disappoint. You may wonder where you might have tasted something like this before – the base and topping are very similar to that of the infamous Daim tart available in many supermarkets the world over (and in those big stores that also happen to sell Swedish bookcases). Add melted Daim and extra chocolate on top, and it all falls into place. This cake is wonderfully gluten-free, too.

200 g/2 cups whole almonds

160 g/1¹/₃ cups icing/confectioners' sugar

5 egg whites

a pinch of salt

TOPPING:

5 egg yolks

100 ml/¹/₃ cup plus 1 tablespoon whipping cream

100 g/¹/₂ cup caster/granulated sugar

150 g/1¹/₄ sticks butter, cut into small pieces, at room temperature

milk/semisweet chocolate curls, to decorate

2 x 20-cm/8-inch round cake pans, greased and lined with baking parchment

SERVES 8

Preheat the oven to 160°C (325°F) Gas 3.

Roughly grind the almonds in a food processor, leaving a few chunkier pieces in there. Combine the ground almonds with the icing/confectioners' sugar and set aside.

In a stand mixer (or using a hand-held whisk), beat the egg whites with a pinch of salt until lightly stiff. Add the ground almond mixture and gently fold in until incorporated.

Pour the mixture into the prepared pans and bake in the preheated oven for around 35–40 minutes or until light brown and a skewer inserted into the middle comes out clean. Turn out carefully onto a wire rack and leave to cool completely.

Meanwhile, make the topping. Put the egg yolks, whipping cream and caster/granulated sugar into a saucepan over a low heat. Bring just to the boil, whisking constantly – as soon as you see the first bubble, quickly take the pan off the heat. To check the mixture is thick enough, dip a spoon in it, then run your finger through the back of the spoon; if the line stays, the mixture is ready.

Leave the mixture to cool to room temperature. Then slowly beat in the room-temperature butter using a hand-held electric whisk, a little at a time, until you have a nice thick, glossy topping.

Spread ²/₃ of the topping mixture onto the first almond base, add the top layer of almond cake and spread the remaining topping on the top. Decorate with chocolate curls and serve chilled and sliced.

Toscatårta
TOSCA CAKE

Said to be named after the Puccini opera, the Tosca cake is one of the most well-loved Nordic cakes. It started appearing in Swedish cookbooks in the 1930s, but some say the cake actually has its origins in Norway. Rather than start any cross-border disagreements, let's just celebrate the cake as a general Nordic triumph – a delicious love story between almonds and buttery caramel. Prepare to be seduced.

200 g/7 oz. marzipan (at least 50% almond content)

200 g/1³/₄ cups icing/ confectioners' sugar

200 g/1³/₄ sticks butter, melted and cooled

4 eggs

150 g/1 cup plus 2 tablespoons plain/all-purpose flour or cake flour

50 g/¹/₃ cup cornflour/ cornstarch

1 teaspoon baking power

1 teaspoon vanilla sugar OR extract OR use the seeds from 1 vanilla pod/bean

¹/₂ teaspoon salt

TOPPING:

75 ml/¹/₃ cup double/heavy cream

60 g/¹/₃ cup caster/ granulated sugar

75 ml/¹/₄ cup runny honey

75 g/³/₄ stick butter

75 g/¹/₄ cup flaked/slivered almonds

pouring cream or ice cream, to serve (optional)

a 23-cm/9-inch springform/ springclip or round cake pan, greased and lined with baking parchment

SERVES 8

Preheat the oven to 180°C (350°F) Gas 4.

Coarsely grate the marzipan into a bowl or stand mixer. Add the icing/confectioners' sugar and beat well using the whisk attachment or a hand-held electric whisk. Beat in the cooled melted butter. Add the eggs, one by one, ensuring each addition is completely incorporated and scraping down the sides of the bowl if needed.

Sift togther all the dry ingredients and fold into the mixture until incorporated. Pour the mixture into the prepared pan and bake in the preheated oven for around 35–40 minutes or until golden brown and firm to the touch. A skewer inserted into the middle should come out clean. Turn the cake out onto a wire rack and leave to cool.

To make the topping, put all the ingredients apart from the almonds in a saucepan over a high heat. Beat with a balloon whisk until the mixture starts to separate from the sides of the pan. (Beat too little and it will not set, beat too much and it will be rock hard, so really keep an eye on it.) As soon as it stops sticking to the sides, remove from the heat, stir in the flaked/slivered almonds and pour over the cake.

Place the cake under a hot grill/broiler for 5–7 minutes to brown the topping but watch it doesn't go too dark. Serve warm with pouring cream on the side, if you wish.

Ostkaka med hjortron
BAKED CHEESECAKE WITH CLOUDBERRIES

Cloudberries look a bit like plump orange raspberries, but the taste is unlike any other berry on the planet. Because of their short season, most cloudberries are made into jam/jelly – and this is usually the only way most people can get hold of them. We love a New York-style baked cheesecake at the café, but admittedly it is not very Scandinavian. It seemed obvious to combine it with our favourite berry to create this amazing New York-meets-Scandi-style treat.

200 g/7 oz. plain biscuits/cookies (I use malted milk or digestives)

75 g/³⁄₄ stick butter, melted

740 g/4 cups full-fat cream cheese

150 g/³⁄₄ cup caster/granulated sugar

2 teaspoons vanilla sugar OR extract OR use the seeds from 1 vanilla pod/bean

1 teaspoon grated lemon zest

2 teaspoons freshly squeezed lemon juice

3 eggs plus 3 egg yolks

TOPPING 1:

300 ml/³⁄₄ cup sour cream

1 tablespoon caster/granulated sugar

1 teaspoon vanilla sugar OR extract OR use the seeds from 1 vanilla pod/bean

TOPPING 2:

140 g/¹⁄₂ cup cloudberry jam/jelly plus fresh or frozen cloudberries if you have them, to decorate

a 23-cm/9-inch springform/springclip pan (ideally leak-proof), greased and base lined with baking parchment

a large, deep roasting pan

SERVES 12

Preheat the oven to 180°C (350°F) Gas 4.

Prepare the springform/springclip pan, then wrap foil around the outside to form a leakproof seal. Place the springform/springclip pan in the large, deep roasting pan.

Crush the biscuits/cookies to crumbs (either with a rolling pin or in a food processor) and mix with the melted butter. Press the mixture evenly into the base of the prepared springform/springclip pan.

Pulse the cream cheese in the food processor for 30 seconds to break up any lumps, then tip into a mixing bowl. Add the sugar, vanilla and lemon zest and juice and whisk to combine fully. Add the eggs and whisk again until just combined, taking care not to overbeat.

Pour the mixture onto the biscuit/cookie base. Pour water into the roasting pan to come halfway up the side of the cheesecake pan to form a bain-marie.

Bake for 45–50 minutes on the middle shelf. The cheesecake is done when it wobbles ever so slightly in the middle. Remove the cheesecake but leave the oven on.

Meanwhile, make topping 1: combine the sour cream, sugar and vanilla then pour over the cheesecake and bake for a further 8–10 minutes. Leave the cheesecake to cool in the oven with the door ajar for an hour, then leave to chill in the refrigerator for at least 4 hours.

Using a knife or metal spatula, carefully loosen the sides of the cake from the pan, then open the springform/springclip. It is easiest to serve on the actual base, so don't worry about removing that.

For topping 2, gently heat the jam/jelly mixed with a small splash of water in a saucepan. When warm (not hot), pour over the cake and spread carefully to cover. If you have extra cloudberries, decorate with these too. Leave to cool, then chill again in the refrigerator so the jam can set before serving.

On long walks along the harbour on the west coast of Sweden, the fresh snow is crunchy underneath heavy boots.

LITTLE
FANCY CAKES

As a child, I could often be found outside the local bakery with my little nose pressed firmly up against the window, trying to catch a glimpse of all the fancy cream cakes. I swear I could almost taste them through the glass. For those days when ordinary cake just won't do, here's a selection of some special cakes to make at home.

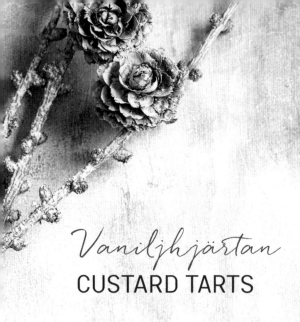

Vaniljhjärtan
CUSTARD TARTS

From Portugal's *pastel de nata* to England's custard tart, most countries have their own version of a pastry cream tart. It's not hard to understand why: firstly, it uses up any leftover pastry cream, and secondly, they are the perfect small bite to accompany a cup of coffee. In Sweden, custard tarts are baked in heart-shaped cases, known as *vaniljhjärtan* – vanilla hearts. In Denmark, they are known as *linser* and baked in round cases.

1 portion of Sweet Shortcrust Pastry Dough (see page 14)

1 portion of Pastry Cream (see page 14)

plain/all-purpose flour and icing/confectioners' sugar for dusting

a pastry/cookie cutter or glass

a 12-hole Yorkshire pudding pan, shallow muffin pan or individual heart-shaped pans, greased with melted butter

MAKES 12–14 VANILLA HEARTS OR 1 YORKSHIRE PUDDING/MUFFIN TRAYFUL (15–18)

Preheat the oven to 180°C (350°F) Gas 4.

Roll out half the sweet shortcrust pastry dough on a lightly floured surface. You want a thickness of around 2–3 mm/$\frac{1}{8}$ inch. Use a pastry/cookie cutter or glass to stamp out the closest size rounds for the pan(s) you have chosen. Line the greased pan(s) neatly with the pastry.

Pour the prepared pastry cream into the pastry bases to fill $\frac{2}{3}$ of the way up.

Roll out the other half of the pastry and cut out lids for the tarts – you will need a very slightly larger sized cutter for this. Dampen the edges of the pastry lids with a little water and add to the tarts, sealing them well. Make sure that the lids fit firmly on the cakes or the pastry cream will seep out during baking. Trim away any leftover pastry.

Bake in the preheated oven for around 20–22 minutes for smaller tarts and 22 mins + for larger shapes, or until they start to turn brown around the edges. Remove from the oven and leave to cool in the pans before carefully lifting out.

Dust with icing/confectioners' sugar before serving.

Napoleonshatte
NAPOLEON HATS

During the 1850s in Denmark, coffee and cake was high fashion – and many of the traditional konditor cakes stem from that time. During that era, we also named a lot of cakes after Napoleon – and his hat is still one of the most iconic and popular Danish cakes today. Every baker worth his salt is likely to have these displayed proudly in their shop window.

1/2 **portion of Sweet Shortcrust Pastry Dough (see page 14)**

250 g/9 oz. store-bought 50% almond content marzipan, grated (or see page 15 for basic recipe)

1 egg white

80 g/1/3 cup plus 2 teaspoons caster/granulated sugar

100 g/3 1/2 oz. 70% dark/bittersweet chocolate, tempered

a baking sheet, greased and lined with baking parchment

an 8 cm/3 1/4 inch round pastry/cookie cutter

MAKES 15

Preheat the oven to 180°C (350°F) Gas 4.

Roll out the pastry on a lightly floured surface to around 2–3 mm/ 1/8inch in thickness. Using the pastry/cookie cutter, stamp out 15 circles.

In a stand mixer or using a wooden spoon and mixing bowl, combine the grated marzipan with the egg white and caster/granulated sugar to form a sticky mass. Roll the mixture into balls weighing around 20 g/3/4 oz. each.

Place a round ball of marzipan in the middle of each pastry circle, then press three of the sides up at the same time to form what looks like Napoleon's hat. Place on the lined baking sheet.

Bake in the preheated oven for around 10–11 minutes or until the pastry turns golden brown. Leave to cool completely on a wire rack.

Coat the base of the cooled 'hats' in a thin layer of tempered chocolate and allow to dry upside down on greaseproof paper.

Note: If you are unsure of how to temper chocolate, use this cheat's method: chop the chocolate and melt half in the microwave or in a heatproof bowl set over a pan of barely simmering water. Do not let the base of the bowl touch the water. When the chocolate is completely melted, remove from the heat and immediately add the other half. Stir together until everything is melted. Your chocolate is now ready to use.

Fragilité

HAZELNUT AND MOCHA SQUARE

This delightful Danish invention evolved at the beginning of the 1900s, back when the Danes were influenced by anything fanciful and French. It's made with meringue – hence the 'fragile' name. You can make the bases with ground hazelnuts or almonds, and you can vary the buttercream filling too. Not into coffee? Omit it and add cocoa to make an intensely chocolatey buttercream. Want a more summery version? Add fresh berries and vanilla buttercream.

MERINGUE BASE:

100 g/^{3}/$_4$ cup hazelnuts

5 egg whites

200 g/1^3/$_4$ cups icing/
confectioners' sugar

BUTTERCREAM:

170 g/^{3}/$_4$ cup plus 1^1/$_2$
tablespoons caster/
granulated sugar

3 tabespoons strong
espresso coffee, cooled

250 g/2^1/$_4$ sticks butter,
softened

1 egg yolk

50 g/2 oz. dark/bittersweet
chocolate, melted

a little extra melted butter,
to grease baking parchment

icing/confectioners' sugar,
to dust

35 x 25-cm/14 x 9^3/$_4$-inch
rectangular baking pan,
greased and lined with
baking parchment

SERVES 5–6

Preheat the oven to 150°C (300°F) Gas 2. Brush a little melted butter onto the baking parchment to help with the release of the meringue.

In a food processor, grind the hazelnuts to a relatively fine and even consistency, making sure no big pieces remain.

Beat the egg whites until stiff in a stand mixer or using a hand-held electric whisk. Add the icing/confectioners' sugar, bit by bit, and whisk until stiff. Fold in the ground hazelnuts.

Spoon the mixture out evenly into the baking pan and level the surface. Pop into the preheated oven to bake for about 45 minutes. It should be baked through but not brown.

Meanwhile, prepare the buttercream. Add the caster/granulated sugar and 100 ml/^{1}/$_3$ cup plus 1 tablespoon water to a saucepan set over medium-high heat, and bring to a bubbly boil. Add the strong espresso coffee and remove from the heat. Leave to cool until just finger-warm.

Combine the softened butter, lukewarm coffee mixture and egg yolk in a bowl and mix together until they start to bind. This may take several minutes, especially if your coffee mixture has gone a bit too cold. Stir in the melted chocolate to form a smooth buttercream.

Once the meringue base has baked and cooled down, remove it from the pan and peel away the baking parchment. Very carefully cut the sides even, then cut into 3 equal rectangles.

To assemble the cake, take the first meringue rectangle and place on your serving plate. Spread over a layer of buttercream. Put the second layer on top, then add another layer of buttercream. Add the top cake layer. Ensure all sides are lined up and even. Dust the top liberally with icing/confectioners' sugar. Leave for at least an hour to soften before very carefully slicing with a serrated knife into 5–6 squares. Any pressure and the filling comes out, so be careful.

Lakridskys

LIQUORICE MERINGUE KISSES

These little meringue kisses are perfect for people who love salty liquorice (most Nordic folk, then). You can get hold of liquorice powder online or in specialist shops – but always go for the good-quality stuff; it really does make a difference. If you are not a fan of liquorice, freeze-dried raspberry powder works as a substitute.

3 egg whites
150 g/³/₄ cup caster/superfine sugar
¹/₂ teaspoon cornflour/cornstarch
¹/₂ teaspoon lemon juice
1 teaspoon raw liquorice powder plus 1 teaspoon for decoration

black food colouring, for piping (optional)

2 baking sheets, greased and lined with baking parchment

a disposable piping/pastry bag

MAKES 40

Preheat the oven to 100°C (215°F) ¹/₄ Gas.

Beat the egg whites on high speed in the clean bowl of a stand mixer or using a hand-held electric whisk. Once the whites begin to stiffen, start to add the sugar, bit by bit. Keep whisking for several minutes until the sugar is fully incorporated and the mixture has formed very stiff peaks.

Add the cornflour/cornstarch and lemon juice and whisk again. Lastly, fold in the liquorice powder.

Paint the inside of the disposable piping/pastry bag with streaks of black food colouring using a pastry brush, reaching right down the length of the bag. Spoon in the meringue mixture and snip the end off the piping/pastry bag.

Pipe mini meringues onto the lined baking sheets (around 2.5 cm/1 inch in diameter). The black food colouring will make a pretty stripy pattern on your meringues.

Sprinkle a little liquorice powder on top of each 'kiss', then bake in the preheated oven for around 40–45 minutes. Turn off the heat and allow to cool down inside the oven for a few minutes before removing.

Eat the kisses on their own or on top of vanilla ice cream, with extra liquorice syrup.

Flødeboller
MALLOW FLUFF CAKES

One of the things that homesick Danes ask for the most at the café are these lovely little soft mallow cakes. Back in Denmark, *flødeboller* have a welcome place at kids' birthday parties, on top of ice cream and as a special treat with an afternoon cup of coffee.

200 g/7 oz. store-bought marzipan with 50% almond content (or see basic recipe on page 15)

MALLOW FILLING:

75 g/$^1/_4$ cup liquid glucose

150 g/$^3/_4$ cup caster/superfine sugar plus 1 extra tablespoon

1 teaspoon freshly squeezed lemon juice

seeds from $^1/_2$ vanilla pod/bean OR 1 teaspoon vanilla extract

100 g/3$^1/_2$ oz. egg whites (do weigh them)

a pinch of salt

CHOCOLATE COATING:

200 g/7 oz. dark/bittersweet chocolate, broken into pieces (I use 70% Valrhona, but a milk chocolate will also give a lovely light result

1 teaspoon vegetable oil (optional)

freeze-dried raspberries, sprinkles or desiccated/dried shredded coconut, to decorate

2 baking sheets, greased and lined with baking parchment

a 4-cm/1$^1/_2$-inch round pastry/cookie cutter

a sugar thermometer

a large piping/pastry bag, fitted with a plain nozzle/tip

MAKES 18–20

Preheat the oven to 180°C (350°F) Gas 4.

Roll out the marzipan to 3 mm/$^1/_8$ inch thickness and stamp out 18–20 small, even thin discs with the pastry/cookie cutter.

Bake in the preheated oven for around 10 minutes or until golden. Leave to cool completely. They will remain soft in the middle.

To make the mallow filling, combine the liquid glucose, 150 g/$^3/_4$ cup caster/superfine sugar, lemon juice and vanilla pod/bean seeds with 50 ml/3$^1/_2$ tablespoons water in a saucepan. Bring to the boil and, using a sugar thermometer, keep heating until you reach 117–118°C/244–245°F. Be aware that if your syrup does not reach this temperature, the mallow will not set correctly. Remove from the heat with care.

Meanwhile, beat the egg whites with the salt until on low–medium speed until they start to combine and froth, using a stand mixer or a hand-held electric whisk. Add the remaining tablespoon of sugar and keep whisking. Increase the speed to high and add the warm syrup in a very thin stream. Once combined, beat for a further for 8–10 minutes. It does take this long to get the thick, stiff peaky mallow.

Add the mallow filling to the piping/pastry bag and carefully pipe a swirl of mallow onto each marzipan base, leaving a bit of the edge free. Aim to have a good high top on each mallow (approx. 4–5 cm/1$^1/_2$ inches). Leave to set for an hour at room temperature or speed up the process by refrigerating.

Temper the chocolate in your usual manner. If you are unsure of how to temper chocolate, see the note on page 97. Add an optional drop of vegetable oil to the warm tempered chocolate for an extra-thin finish.

To coat, place a mallow bun on a wire rack, resting over a bowl. Spoon over the tempered chocolate, then transfer with a spatula to a different tray to dry. Repeat until you have completed the batch. You may have to pour excess chocolate back from the drip bowl to use again. Decorate with freeze-dried raspberries, sprinkles or desiccated/dried shredded coconut. Leave to cool and set before eating.

Fancy fika

Scandinavian baking in general is quite wholesome and largely focused around the home. There is another side though – the pastries and fancy cakes, admired in bakery windows across Scandinavia. My eight-year-old self found it impossible to pass by a bakery without ensuring the mark of my squashed nose was left against the polished glass window. These are the types of cake we tend not to attempt at home, but I want to show you that actually they are not as difficult as people think, and so worth a little bit of extra effort.

At ScandiKitchen, we love combining the idea of wholesome fika (meeting up for a coffee or tea and a bite of something sweet to eat, see pages 74–75 for a full description) with the traditional idea of English afternoon tea (well, when in London...). We also love to marry the idea of the fancier afternoon fika with sturdy buns and breads to ensure there is always a bit of what you fancy when you drop by.

During the 1700s many foreign bakers brought new spices and recipes across to Scandinavia, which in turn influenced our baking style. Later, with the rise of unions in Denmark, it became law that a proportion of bakers needed to be Danish and outside influence on our traditional recipes stopped for a while. During the 1850s there was a strike in Denmark by all bakery workers, which meant the master bakers had

to import help from as far away as Austria. When this overseas help arrived, they brought with them a wealth of diverse knowledge and skills, most notably the Viennese method of making pastry. Suddenly, the most delicate pastries in Denmark were redefined by new *plundergebäcken* methods (dough wrapped in butter and rolled 27 times to form paper-thin layers of buttery puffed pastry). When the Austrian bakers went home, the Danes continued to develop this new breed of pastry – eventually resulting in what is now known all over the world as 'Danish pastry'.

In Scandinavia, this type of pastry is now known as *Wienerbrød* (Vienna bread). You can find our delicious Danish pastry recipes in the Breads & Batters chapter pages 142 and 145 as well as the giant Danish pastry Kringle on page 126.

Along with the influence of the Austrian bakers in Denmark at that time, meeting up at cake houses for coffee and tea became ever more popular in fancy circles, and so the need for more elaborate cakes arose. It was the height of fashion to meet up and eat delicate pastries and cream cakes such as Sarah Bernhardt cakes on page 113 (the famous actress had this cake named after her on her visit to Copenhagen), and the Napoleon's Hat cakes on page 97.

An obsession with fancy eclairs and indulgent cream-based cakes took hold and became very much the 'in thing' to eat at that time.

Although quite a few of these recipes originated in Denmark, they spread across Scandinavia and other parts of Europe. Many of the cakes originally made famous or invented in Denmark are available throughout Scandinavia today, although sometimes with slightly different names and regional variations. The Sarah Bernhardt cakes, for example, are called *Biskvier* in Sweden and have a slightly different filling, but the original idea and shape are the same.

People often ask me why Scandinavians are considered so healthy when we have such a sweet tooth. It is all about balance. You won't find many Danes who eat a pastry every morning, because that wouldn't be *tilpasseligt* (or *lagom* – just enough, not too much or too little). Instead, they'll have them for breakfast on a Sunday or a special occasion.

Kartoffelkager
POTATO CAKES

Let's get one thing straight: there are no hidden potatoes in these cakes. The name stems from their look, not the ingredients. This type of cream cake originated in Denmark, where it first made an appearance in the early 1900s. There are two varieties – one has a sponge base and the other is choux pastry. For me, the choux pastry wins every time for the lightness.

CHOUX BUNS:

170 g/scant 1¼ cups white strong/bread flour

½ teaspoon salt

¼ teaspoon baker's ammonia (see page 36 for further information; these will still work without, it just makes the pastry extra crisp)

125 g/1⅛ sticks butter

1 tablespoon caster/granulated sugar

4–5 eggs, mixed together and placed in a small jug/pitcher

FILLING:

250 ml/1 cup whipping cream

¼ portion of Pastry Cream (see page 14)

TOPPING:

300–400 g/10–14 oz. store-bought marzipan with 50% almond content (or see basic recipe on page 15)

icing/confectioners' sugar and cocoa powder, for dusting

2 baking sheets, greased and lined with baking parchment

a large piping/pastry bag fitted with large plain nozzle/tip (optional)

a 5 cm/2 inch round pastry/cookie cutter

MAKES 25

Preheat the oven to 200°C (400°C) Gas 6.

Sift together the flour, salt and baker's ammonia (if using).

Put the butter and sugar into a saucepan with 275 ml/1¼ cups water and melt together over a low heat. Add the flour and stir with a spatula until incorporated and the mixture lets go of the sides of the pan. Remove from the heat and let cool for a few minutes.

Start to add the eggs a little at a time to the cooled dough, beating well between each addition until well combined. You may not need all the eggs. You want to end up with a smooth mixture that still holds if piped, but drops from the spoon in about 3–4 seconds. Be patient and keep mixing after each egg addition to see if you need more.

Spoon or pipe out around 25 buns of equal generous size onto the prepared baking sheets. They will rise and puff up slightly, so space them well apart. I usually don't pipe the choux pastry because I like a rustic finish, but it is up to you, of course.

Pop in the preheated oven and immediately reduce the heat to 180°C (350°F) Gas 4. Bake for 20–25 minutes until well risen and golden brown. Try not to open the door to the oven during the baking time. To make sure the buns are cooked, take one out and see if it collapses. If it sinks, bake the buns for a few more minutes.

Remove from the oven and poke a small hole in each bun to let the steam escape. Leave to cool down completely.

No more than two hours before serving, whip the cream to stiff peaks, then fold in the pastry cream. Cut each bun open and pipe in a generous amount of filling to taste.

Roll out the marzipan on a surface lightly dusted with icing/confectioners' sugar. Stamp out shapes to fit over the top of the choux pastry balls using the round cutter. Add the marzipan circles to the top of the potato cakes and dust with cocoa powder before serving.

Hindbærsnitter
RASPBERRY SQUARES

I used to eat these on the way home from school when I was a kid. I'd save up the leftover change from lunch money and buy *hindbærsnitter* as often as I could afford to. My kids, Astrid and Elsa, love these too and they are always a welcome addition to the school cake sale table. Show me the child who doesn't love frosting, jam/jelly and biscuit – it's the sweet and simple things that please the little ones the most.

1 portion of Sweet Shortcrust Pastry Dough (see page 14)
200 g/^{1}/$_2$ cup good-quality raspberry jam/jelly
300 g/2^1/$_2$ cups icing/confectioners' sugar
1–3 tablespoons hot water
sprinkles, to decorate

2 baking sheets, greased and lined with baking parchment

MAKES 12–16

Preheat the oven to 180°C (350°F) Gas 4.

Split the sweet shortcrust pastry dough into two equal portions and roll into 2 evenly sized squares, around 3 mm/^{1}/$_8$ inch thick. Each one should be around 30 x 30 cm/11 x 11 inches. Ensure the shapes are the same size as you will be layering them later.

Put the pastry squares on the prepared baking sheets. Prick the surfaces with a fork to prevent air bubbles forming as they bake. Pop in the preheated oven to bake for about 10–12 minutes or until slightly golden. Remove from the oven and set aside to cool on a wire rack.

On one of the cooled pastry sheets, spread a generous, even layer of the raspberry jam/jelly. Very carefully, slide the other piece of pastry on top so that it sits exactly on top of the base. Handle delicately, as the pastry can break quite easily.

Mix the icing/confectioners' sugar with hot water to form a smooth paste. The amount of water you will need varies depending on your sugar. If the paste is too thick, add a few drops more water. Too thin, add a bit more icing/confectioners' sugar. Aim for the consistency of runny honey. Spread the icing/frosting on top of the pastry to evenly cover. Top with sprinkles and leave to dry.

Using a very sharp knife, cut the edges off the pastry to make straight sides. Cut into 12 large or 16 small equal pieces to serve.

Medaljer
MEDALS

These medals hold great memories for me. I remember my grandmother loved having her friends over to play cards on a Friday afternoon and sometimes, if it was someone's birthday, they'd stop by the baker's and bring little fancy cakes. All the ladies would sit around in the lounge in the big old house and *hygge*, laugh loudly, play cards and eat cake. There were always leftovers. What kid can resist sweet biscuit cakes with whipped cream? Not me.

$^1/_2$ **portion of Sweet Shortcrust Pastry Dough (see page 14)**

$^1/_4$ **portion of Pastry Cream (see page 14)**

FILLING:

150 ml/$^2/_3$ cup whipping cream

1 tablespoon icing/confectioners' sugar

a pinch of vanilla sugar or a drop of vanilla extract

FROSTING:

60 g/$^1/_2$ cup icing/confectioners' sugar

15 g/$^1/_2$ oz. cocoa powder

sprinkles and/or small berries, to garnish

a 7–8-cm/2$^3/_4$–3$^1/_2$ inch round pastry/cookie cutter

a baking sheet, greased and lined with baking parchment

a piping/pastry bag fitted with a star nozzle/tip

MAKES 10–12

Remove the sweet shortcrust pastry from the refrigerator a while before using.

Preheat the oven to 200°C (400°F) Gas 6.

Roll out the pastry on a lightly floured surface to about 2–3 mm/$^1/_8$–$^1/_4$ inch thick. Cut out 24 circles using the round pastry/cookie cutter and place them on the prepared baking sheet.

Bake for about 6–8 minutes in the preheated oven or until just a little bit browned. Leave to cool on a wire rack.

Beat the whipping cream with the icing/confectioners' sugar and vanilla until stiff. Set aside.

To make the frosting, mix the icing/confectioners' sugar with the cocoa powder, then add 2–3 tablespoons hot water and stir. You may need to add more water, but do so slowly so that it does not get too runny. You want a thick yet spreadable frosting.

Spread around a teaspoon each of frosting on top of half of the pastry circles. Use the back of the spoon to neatly spread toward the edges. Before the frosting sets, add the sprinkles.

Put a large teaspoon of pastry cream in the middle of each remaining bare pastry circle. Spoon the whipped cream into the piping/pastry bag and pipe a neat circle of whipped cream around the pastry cream. Add the iced top layer and garnish with another swirl of whipped cream and small fresh berries, if desired. Serve chilled and eat with a pastry fork.

Tip: Add a delicious fruity edge by combining a bit of puréed raspberry with the whipping cream.

Biskvier
SARAH BERNHARDT CAKES

Back in the day it was all the rage to name cakes after famous people, so when French actress Sarah Bernhardt visited Denmark in 1911, a local Copenhagen *konditor* created a new cake and named it after her. Then the Swedes came along and decided to make it slightly differently and called it *biskvier* instead. This recipe is a middle-ground between the two versions; it tastes great and just happens to be gluten-free, too. Plus, now I won't offend either country. There is raw yolk in the filling, but you can replace this with a dash of milk if you prefer.

200 g/7 oz. store-bought marzipan with 50% almond content (or see basic recipe on page 15)

70 g/ $^1/_2$ cup icing/confectioners' sugar

$^1/_2$ egg white

FILLING:

120 g/1 cup icing/confectioners' sugar

150 g/1 $^1/_4$ sticks butter, at room temperature

1 teaspoon vanilla sugar, extract OR use the seeds seeds from $^1/_2$ vanilla pod/bean

1 egg yolk

75 g/3 oz. 70% dark/bittersweet chocolate, melted

1 teaspoon cocoa powder

a few teaspoons cold, strong espresso coffee (optional)

COATING:

125 g/4$^1/_2$ oz. 70% dark/bittersweet chocolate, tempered (see page 97)

freeze-dried raspberries or popping candy, to decorate

a baking sheet, lined with baking parchment

a piping/pastry bag fitted with a plain nozzle/tip

MAKES 15

Preheat the oven to 180°C (350°F) Gas 4.

First, make the bases. Mix the marzipan with the icing/confectioners' sugar and add the half an egg white. Mix into a pliable dough.

Using damp hands, separate and mould the dough into 15 little round balls of around 20 g/1 oz. each. Arrange on the prepared baking sheet and press down slightly to flatten each one to around $^1/_2$ cm/$^1/_4$ inch in height.

Bake in the preheated oven for around 10–12 minutes or until golden around the edges. Leave to cool on a wire rack.

Meanwhile, make the filling. In a stand mixer with the whisk attachment (or using a hand-held electric whisk), beat the icing/confectioners' sugar, butter and vanilla on high speed until fully incorporated. Add the egg yolk and whisk again. Finally, beat in the melted dark/bittersweet chocolate and cocoa powder. Continue to beat until you have a light, fluffy mixture. Fold in the espresso coffee now, if using.

Using a spatula, cover each cooled marzipan disc with the filling. Traditionally, the filling is added with a knife and shaped a bit like a spinning top, but if you prefer a rounder and neater topping, you can use a piping/pastry bag. Chill the cakes in the refrigerator for 20–30 minutes. When you take them out, use a smooth knife edge to level any messy toppings, so that the chocolate coating will go on smoothly.

When you are ready to cover the biskvier, temper the chocolate to your usual method or see page 97 for instructions.

Dip each *biskvier* in the tempered chocolate and ensure all the filling is covered in a thin layer. Hold the *biski* up to allow excess chocolate to drip away – you don't want it too thick. Decorate with freeze-dried raspberries or popping candy before allowing to dry.

CELEBRATION CAKES

Scandinavians love to celebrate. It is a great excuse for family and friends to get together and to share a bit of something sweet. Here you will find a selection of larger cakes perfect for sharing with loved ones on those days that are extra special: birthdays, anniversaries, national days and even weddings.

Kransekage

ALMOND RING CELEBRATION CAKE

This is the ultimate celebration cake in both Norway and Denmark, served at weddings, christenings, big birthdays, national days and more. It is not very often attempted at home as it can be fiddly to get perfect, presentation-wise. When done right it is, however, a total showstopper in all senses of the word. You can now buy the *kransekage* rings online from specialist and some high-street shops, but it is possible to make the cake freehand, too. *Kransekage* is only ever decorated with simple white icing/frosting, flags and maybe a few streamers for New Year. At weddings, the figurines of the couple are placed on top of the cake.

2–3 egg whites (no more than 100 g/3¹/₂ oz (do weigh them)

500 g/1 lb. 60% almond content store-bought marzipan (or see page 15 for basic recipe), grated

100 g/1 cup ground almonds

100 g/1 cup icing/confectioners' sugar, plus extra for rolling

100 g/³/₄ cup caster/superfine sugar

1 teaspoon almond extract

Make sure that your *kransekage* pans (if using) are greased with plenty of cake-release spray, as these cakes are notorious for sticking.

In a bowl, lightly beat the egg whites to a foam using a hand-held electric whisk or the whisk attachment in a stand mixer. Add the ground almonds, icing/confectioners' sugar and caster/superfine sugar and whisk again until you have a smooth paste. Mix in the grated marzipan. Your final mixture will be sticky but you should be able to handle it. Place the paste in a plastic bag and chill in the refrigerator for at least an hour before using.

Cut a piece of the paste and work it with as much icing/confectioners' sugar as needed to make it rollable and roll out the first piece into a long roll with a diameter of 1–1.25 cm/³/₈–¹/₂ inch. Shape the roll to fit inside the first ring in the pan and smooth over where the ends join together neatly. Repeat the process and aim to form 10 perfect sized rings to fit inside the pans. The rolls should be the same width and height exactly, so use a ruler if you want to be sure, and don't rush. The rolls have to be smooth, so keep a glass of water next to you and use damp fingers to help smooth out any bumps. There should be a little bit of paste left over to make a freehand top for your tower. Place on a piece of baking parchment on a baking sheet.

If making the freehand version, your first smallest roll should be 8 cm/3¹/₈ inches long and 1–1.25 cm/³/₈–¹/₂ inch diameter. The next 10.5 cm/4¹/₈ inches long and so on – increasing the length by 2.5 cm/1 inch each time. Connect the rings freehand on top of baking parchment on a baking sheet. If possible double up on baking sheets to give more heat protection to the rings. Again, smooth the connections and bumps out using damp hands and make sure your pieces are all as even and smooth as possible. Don't forget to again make the freehand top for your tower.

ICING/FROSTING:

1/2–1 small egg white

100 g/3/4 cup sifted icing/
confectioners' sugar (add
more as needed)

*1 x set of kransekage
cake pans, liberally greased
with cake-release spray
(or baking sheets if making
freehand)*

*a piping/pastry bag with
a small nozzle/tip (size 2)*

a large serving plate

**MAKES A 10-RING CAKE
TO SERVE 15**

Preheat the oven to 200°C (400°F) Gas 6.

Bake one pan at a time in the middle of the preheated oven, putting the pans on a baking sheet (not directly on the oven rack). They will need around 10–15 minutes each, until they have a light golden sheen.

Remove from the oven and (if using pans) allow the cake to cool completely in the pan before removing. If the cakes are sticking, loosen around the edges with a knife; they are very delicate, so do this carefully. If you have used the freehand method, remove the baking parchment and rings from the baking tray and place onto a colder surface to cool.

To make the icing/frosting, mix together the egg white with the icing/confectioners' sugar, adding more as needed until you achieve an icing that is thick enough to firmly hold its shape, but still light enough to comfortably pipe through a small nozzle/tip (size 2).

To assemble, place the largest bottom cake layer on a serving plate and fill the piping/pastry bag with icing/frosting. Pipe a small circle of icing/frosting on the ring, slightly towards the inside edge, and place the second largest ring on top. Repeat the process with all the rings, until you have a finished tower. Take care after adding each ring to ensure your tower is straight and even from all sides. Finally, fix the top onto the cake.

To decorate, start the flow of the icing/frosting from the inside edge and then immediately pull the nozzle back onto the outside edge in one continuous movement. Continue back and forth, if you need to stop at any point to adjust your nozzle, do so when piping the inside of the ring, as a messy end there will be less visible than the outside. Make sure the lines of icing/frosting are reasonably close together and not in a zig zag.

Alternatively, you can decorate all layers separately then assemble. This allows more control for mistakes, but you will have to handle the cake after icing, which may damage your work.

Decorate with a few cocktail flags or other tasteful Scandi decorations suitable for the occasion. This cake is extremely rich and should be served in small pieces. Therefore, a 10-ring cake is enough for a party of 15, as it is not really a dessert, but more of a petit four- style treat. For a wedding cake, double the ingredients to make the 18-ring cake and it should be enough for at least 30 guests.

Tip: You can freeze the kransekage cake rings for up to 3 months. Take care to place in a container so that they will not get bumped in your freezer. The cake keeps for quite a long time even without freezing, so it's a great one to make in advance, ahead of your celebration.

Prinsesstårta
PRINCESS CAKE

One of the most famous cakes to come out of Sweden, this traditional celebration cake first appeared in 1948 in *The Princesses Cookbook*, authored by Jenny Åkerström, a teacher of Princesses Margaretha, Märtha and Astrid, daughters of Prince Carl. Originally called Green Cake, the name evolved due to the Princesses apparent fondness for it.

1 portion of Layer Cake Bases (see page 12)

1 portion of Pastry Cream (see page 14)

600 ml/2¼ cups whipping cream

2 tablespoons icing/confectioners' sugar

150 g/½ cup good-quality raspberry jam/jelly

200 g/7 oz. green marzipan (store-bought or see recipe on page 15 and add a drop of green food colouring paste, not liquid)

pink and green royal icing or marzipan, for the rose and leaves

icing/confectioners' sugar, for dusting

a piping bag fitted with a star nozzle/tip

SERVES 8–10

Whip the cream with the icing/confectioners' sugar until stiff. Spoon two thirds into a separate bowl. Mix the remaining one third of the whipped cream with the prepared pastry cream.

Make sure your prepared layer cake bases are completely even in size. If not, trim to fit. Place the bottom layer on your chosen serving plate; you won't be able to move the cake once assembled.

Spread the raspberry jam/jelly evenly onto the base layer of the cake, then add half of the pastry cream mixture. Top with the second cake layer. Repeat with the remaining jam/jelly and second helping of the pastry cream mixture. Add the top cake layer.

Using a cake spatula, spread three quarters of the remaining stiffly whipped cream in a thick layer on the top and the sides of the cake. Make sure the cake is covered evenly all over to prevent jam/jelly from seeping out. Some people prefer to shape the cream into a dome; I quite like more of a level top on my princess cake, but it is up to you.

Next, roll out the green marzipan on a surface lightly dusted with icing/confectioners' sugar or over the top of baking parchment (to prevent sticking). Roll out into a large, even circle, big enough to cover the top and sides of the cake (around 35 cm/14 inches + in diameter).

Carefully drape the marzipan on top of the cake and peel back the baking parchment, if using. Pull gently around the edges to bring the marzipan down to cover the cake, taking care not to overstretch. Once the marzipan is smoothed over and touching the base all the way around, trim away the excess. Press the edges gently in at the base.

To make the rose decorations, mould the pink royal icing or marzipan into 2 cm/¾ inch tall teardrop shapes for the inside buds. Then roll out small round petal-shaped pieces of icing around 2 x 2 cm / ¾ x ¾ inch and wrap each one around the bud in layers. Cut the base off and fix the roses on top of the cake. Lastly, roll out the green royal icing or marzipan and cut out leaf shapes to fix by the sides of the rose. Dust with icing/confectioners' sugar before serving.

Chokoladekage med lakridscreme

CHOCOLATE CAKE WITH LIQUORICE GANACHE

Did we tell you that Scandinavians love salty liquorice? This rich chocolate cake is topped with a whipped white chocolate ganache that is flavoured with salty liquorice syrup and powder.

50 g/^{1}/$_2$ cup cocoa powder

100 ml/^{1}/$_3$ cup plus 1 tablespoon whole milk

300 g/2^3/$_4$ sticks butter

400 g/2 cups caster/granulated sugar

3 eggs

300 g/2^1/$_4$ cups plain/all-purpose flour or cake flour

1 teaspoon vanilla sugar OR extract

1 teaspoon bicarbonate of/baking soda

^{1}/$_2$ teaspoon salt

LIQUORICE GANACHE:

250 ml/1 cup double/heavy cream

250 g/8^3/$_4$ oz. good-quality white chocolate, chopped

1 tablespoon salty liquorice syrup, plus extra for drizzling

1 teaspoon liquorice powder

4 x 15–16-cm/6-inch round cake pans, greased and lined with baking parchment

a piping/pastry bag with a star tip/nozzle (optional)

SERVES 10

Make the liquorice ganache first. Bring the double/heavy cream to boiling point in a saucepan. Remove from the heat and add the white chocolate, liquorice syrup and powder. Stir to melt. Leave to cool then chill in the refrigerator for a few hours.

Preheat the oven to 170°C (325°F) Gas 3.

Mix together the cocoa powder with 150 ml/^{2}/$_3$ cup boiling water and stir until smooth. Add the milk to the mixture and stir again. Cool and set aside.

Cream together the butter and sugar until pale and fluffy in a stand mixer or using a hand-held electric whisk. Add the eggs one by one, beating with each addition to fully incorporate. In a separate bowl, sift together the plain/all-purpose or cake flour, vanilla, bicarbonate of/baking soda and salt. Add the flour mixture and the cocoa mixture to the egg mixture alternately while beating continuously on a slow speed just until well incorporated.

Divide the mixture into 4 equal portions (of around 300 g/10^1/$_2$ oz. each). Spoon into the prepared baking pans and spread out evenly. Bake in the middle of the preheated oven for around 15 minutes or until a skewer inserted into the middle comes out just clean. Leave to cool.

Whisk the chilled ganache on high speed until the colour becomes a few shades lighter and the texture becomes light and fluffy. Spread over 3 chocolate cake layers and stack the sponges one on top of the other. Finish with a generous layer of ganache on the top layer (piped if you wish) and drizzle with extra liquorice syrup to decorate.

Kringle

DANISH PASTRY KRINGLE

The name *Kringle* refers to the pretzel shape of this Danish pastry. Actually, the word originates from the Old Norse *kringla*, meaning ring or circle, so it wasn't originally pretzel-shaped at all. We eat kringle for birthdays, parties and at other festive times – I think it's super-festive to have one on the table to share rather than lots of smaller pastries.

1 portion of Danish Pastry (see page 13)

1 portion of Remonce Almond Paste (see page 15)

1 egg mixed with a few tablespoons double/heavy cream, for brushing

50–100 g/^{1}/$_2$–^{3}/$_4$ cup raisins (to taste)

50 g/^{1}/$_4$ cup toasted, roughly chopped hazelnuts

caster/granulated sugar, to dust

icing/confectioners' sugar (optional)

a large baking sheet (big enough to accommodate 40 cm x 40 cm/16 x 16 inches of dough) greased and lined with baking parchment

SERVES 12–15

Roll out the Danish pastry lengthways on a lightly floured surface. Push the sides back in, turn over and roll again. Because the pastry has lots of layers, you have to do it this way or you will ruin the flakiness. When you have a long rectangle of around 50 cm/20 inches, cut it straight down the middle. The kringle is so big that it is easier to make in two pieces. Keep rolling each piece so it becomes longer and thinner, taking care not to disturb the layers. Each piece should end up around 50–55 cm/20–22 inches long and no more than 10 cm/4 inches wide.

Add the remonce in a line down the middle of both pieces and then add the raisins, too. Fold each side onto the remonce to make a long package with the remonce secured in the middle, leaving about 1 cm/^{3}/$_8$ inch exposed.

Trim off the untidy end bits of both pieces of pastry. Carefully curve both pieces of pastry into thick horseshoe shapes and transfer onto the prepared baking sheet so that the ends face each other. Join the ends of each horseshoe together on one side. For the other side, fold one end of pastry up diagonally beneath the other and join. You should end up with a pretzel-like shape. Make the final adjustments to the kringle with your hands. It will rise quite a bit, so make sure the holes are big enough that they won't disapear. Cover with a kitchen cloth and leave to rest for around 20 minutes.

Brush with the egg-cream wash all over, then dust lightly with caster/granulated sugar and sprinkle over the toasted chopped hazelnuts.

Preheat the oven to 180°C (350°F) Gas 4. Note: you may want to place an extra tray at the bottom of your oven to catch any drips of butter.

Bake in the preheated oven for 20–30 minutes. The sugar will melt and make the pastry go brown, so do check if it's cooked through inside. It may need a little longer depending on the thickness of the pastry.

Remove from oven and allow to cool. You can add frosting if you wish, but I think it's nice just dusted with a little icing/confectioners' sugar.

Rugbrødslagkage med kirsebær
RYE BREAD LAYER CAKE WITH CHERRIES

This type of Danish layer cake comes from Sønderjylland in southern Denmark. Here, this cake is known as *brødtort* (bread cake), because the bases are made from finely ground rye bread. The *brødtort* is usually one of the star attractions on the famous elaborate Jutland cake tables (see pages 30–31). I'm always amazed that this recipe hasn't travelled further – even in Denmark, many people have not heard of it. It's truly delicious in an almost wholesome way, although, considering the amount of cream, one is not fooled for long.

5 eggs, separated

150 g/¾ cup caster/granulated sugar

2 tablespoons cornflour/cornstarch

2 tablespoons cocoa powder

2 teaspoons baking powder

a pinch of salt

1 teaspoon vanilla sugar OR extract OR use the seeds from 1 vanilla pod/bean

100 g/1 cup freshly ground almonds (pulsed in a food processer, not as finely as the pre-packaged ones)

150 g/5 oz. stale dark rye bread, finely ground in a food processor

TOPPING AND FILLING:

500 ml/2 cups whipping cream

1 tablespoon icing/confectioners' sugar

a few drops of amaretto, (or almond extract) plus extra, for brushing

100 g/½ cup cherry jam/jelly

300 g/1½ cups fresh cherries, pitted

chocolate shavings, to decorate

3 x 20-cm/8-inch round cake pans, greased and lined with baking parchment

SERVES 8–10

Preheat the oven to 180°C (350°F) Gas 4.

In a stand mixer (or using a hand-held electric whisk), beat the egg yolks with the caster/granulated sugar until pale and thick.

Combine the cornflour/cornstarch, cocoa powder, baking powder and salt together in a separate bowl then sift into the yolk and sugar mixture. Add the vanilla and fold in gently. Lastly, fold in the freshly ground almonds and the rye breadcrumbs.

Whisk the egg whites until stiff (so you can hold the bowl upside down and nothing falls), then fold into the rye bread mixture until combined.

Split the mixture evenly between the three prepared pans and bake in the preheated oven for around 20–25 minutes, or until the cakes are slightly springy to the touch and pull away slightly from the sides of the pans. The cakes will not rise much during baking and this is fine.

Leave to cool for a while in the pans, then carefully turn out onto a wire rack to cool completely.

To make the topping and filling, whip the cream with the icing/confectioners' sugar and a few drops of amaretto or almond extract until stiff.

Arrange the first cake layer on your serving plate, brush with a thin layer of amaretto (if using) and add a thin layer of cherry jam/jelly. Add a quarter of the whipped cream, then arrange half of the cherries on top. Add the second cake layer. Repeat the process with this layer and add the final cake layer on top. Top with the remaining cream and sprinkle liberally with chocolate shavings to decorate.

Winter celebrations

The further north you live in the Nordic countries, the scarcer daylight hours become in winter. When the days close in and the leaves fall off the trees, we prepare for darkness and cold to arrive, but also for the biggest celebration of our year: *jul* (Christmas).

We have many ways of coping with the cold and darkness during the winter months. Our homes are warm and cosy, full of candlelight flickering in every room to encourage the feelings of *hygge* when the snow is falling outside.

I have lived in many different countries and I am yet find people who love Christmas as much Scandinavians. We really celebrate the whole season – especially when it comes to baking. At this time of the year my café becomes a focal point for homesick ex-pat Scandinavians seeking out fellow Scandis to feel Christmas joy with.

The Four Sundays of Advent (the last four Sundays before Christmas) are celebrated with *glögg* (mulled wine) parties, where there is always an abundance of ginger cookies, usually home-baked. These cookies vary regionally – Norwegian *brunkaker* are different to Danish *pebernødder* and Swedish *pepparkakor*.

The 13th December is important across the Nordic countries, and is better known as the day of *Sankta Lucia*. In pagan times, folk thought that the enchantress Lussi would ride through the night and cause chaos and destruction – and

even come down the chimney to take away children! People would stay awake all night to ensure she couldn't harm them. With the coming of Christianity, the occasion changed to commemorate Saint Lucia of Syracuse, and incorporated elements of the winter solstice to mark the bringing of light into the darkness. Today, we get up very early in the morning to watch processions of teenagers wearing white robes carrying candles. And one lucky person plays Lucia – wearing a crown of candlelight. In Sweden and Norway, we eat saffron buns called *lussekatter*, while Danes enjoy *æbleskiver* (see page 157).

Christmas Eve is the main day for celebration, so we don't have to wait until 25th December for presents. While the rest of the Western world has Santa, we have *nisser* or *tomter* – the Christmas gnomes. These resemble the modern Santa with beards and red hats, but they are much smaller and you have to treat them well

all year round if you want to avoid them playing mischief on you.

New Year brings hopes for the year ahead – and with it, several more months of darkness and snow: a perfect excuse for more *hygge* and candlelight. We Scandinavians have a peaceful relationship with snow and cold – it is just part of our year, so we dress for it, accept it and live with it, almost in harmony. ('No such thing as bad weather, only bad clothes,' say all Scandinavian mothers.)

In February, bakeries start to make *semla* (Lent) buns. In Denmark and Norway, we call them *fastelavnsboller*. All the way up to Shrove Tuesday, we eat these buns and on Shrove Tuesday we'll probably have two. Then comes Lent, *semlor* buns disappear and we begin to focus on Easter, the return of light, getting in the last bit of skiing before the snow disappears, and we start to dream of lighter, warmer days.

Budapesttårta
BUDAPEST ROLL

This is my partner Jonas's favourite cake. He doesn't normally have much of a sweet tooth, but this is the one he requests for his birthday. The name Budapest has nothing to do with Hungary – this version of the cake was actually invented in Sweden. I have to admit, this cake is nostalgic for me: as a child of the eighties, there wasn't a party without a meringue roll full of canned fruit. I do, however, really prefer to use fresh mandarins when they are in season.

6 egg whites (200 g/7 oz.)
a pinch of salt
325 g/1^1/$_2$ cups plus
2 tablespoons caster/
granulated sugar
30 g/^{1}/$_4$ cup cornflour/
cornstarch
1 teaspoon white wine
vinegar
150 g/1^1/$_4$ cups toasted
hazelnuts, roughly ground
in a food processor

MANDARIN FILLING:
300 ml/1^1/$_4$ cups double/
heavy cream
1 teaspoon icing/
confectioners' sugar
1 teaspoon vanilla sugar,
extract OR use the seeds
from 1 vanilla pod/bean
300 g/10^1/$_2$ oz. fresh
mandarins (approx. 3–4)

TOPPING:
50 g/2 oz. dark/bittersweet
chocolate, melted
25 g/^{3}/$_4$ oz. toasted chopped
hazelnuts

a 25 x 35-cm/9 ^{3}/$_4$ x 14-inch
Swiss roll/jelly pan/baking
pan, greased and lined with
baking parchment

a large piping/pastry bag
fitted with a plain nozzle/tip
(optional)

SERVES 8–10

Preheat the oven to 180°C (350°F) Gas 4.

In a very clean bowl, beat the egg whites with a teeny pinch of salt in a stand mixer (or using a hand-held electric whisk) until lightly stiff. Start adding the caster/granulated sugar, bit by bit. Keep whisking until you reach stiff peak stage, this may take a few minutes. Add the cornflour/cornstarch and white wine vinegar and beat again to incorporate.

Fold in the roughly ground hazelnuts. Fill the piping/pastry bag with the meringue mixture. Pipe into the prepared pan in an even layer. Alternatively, spoon the mixture into the pan and spread evenly.

Bake for around 25–30 minutes until the meringue is firm, slightly cracked on top and lightly browned. Leave to cool in the pan for about 10 minutes.

Cut a large piece of baking parchment slightly larger than the pan and place on the worktop. Carefully turn the meringue out onto the baking parchment and let cool completely.

Meanwhile, whip the cream for the filling with the icing/confectioners' sugar and vanilla until stiff. Peel the mandarins and remove the pips and as much membrane as possible. Chop the flesh into small pieces.

Peel away the parchment paper from the cold meringue. If it is difficult to remove, brush the paper with a little water. Spread an even layer of whipped cream on top of the meringue and then add the mandarin pieces. Very carefully roll up the meringue lengthways, as tightly and neatly as possible, using the baking parchment to help you.

Transfer to a serving plate, making sure the seam is underneath. Tidy up any spills of cream. Drizzle the dark/bittersweet melted chocolate across the top in a messy pattern, then sprinkle with the toasted chopped hazelnuts. Chill in the refrigerator until ready to serve and slice into portions at the table.

Othello lagkage
OTHELLO LAYER CAKE

Named after Shakespeare's Othello, this luxurious layer cake is one of the most popular at Danish bakeries. Indulgent and fancy, it is perfect for serving up at special occasions.

1 portion of Layer Cake Bases (see page 12)
$^1/_2$ portion of Pastry Cream (see page 14)

ALMOND LAYER:
2 egg whites
75 g/$^3/_4$ cup ground almonds
50 g/$^1/_4$ cup caster/granulated sugar
100 g/$^3/_4$ cup plus 1$^1/_2$ tablespoons icing/confectioners' sugar
1 teaspoon almond extract

FILLING:
400 ml/1$^1/_2$ cups whipping cream
1 tablespoon icing/confectioners' sugar
75–100 g/$^1/_4$–$^1/_3$ cup good-quality raspberry jam/jelly

ICING/FROSTING:
100 g/$^3/_4$ cup plus 1$^1/_2$ tablespoons icing/confectioners' sugar
50 g/2 oz. good-quality 70% dark/bittersweet chocolate, melted and still warm
150 g/5 oz. store-bought good-quality marzipan (or see basic recipe page 15), to decorate

a large baking sheet, greased and lined with baking parchment

a piping/pastry bag fitted with a plain nozzle/tip

SERVES 8–10

Preheat the oven to 180°C (350°F) Gas 4.

To make the almond layer, whisk the egg whites until stiff, add the other ingredients and mix until smooth. Spread the almond mixture into a circle the same size as the cake bases (20 cm/8 inches diameter) on the baking parchment on the baking sheet. Bake in the preheated oven for around 15 minutes until golden brown. Leave to cool.

Whip the cream until stiff with the icing/confectioners' sugar. Reserve 1 heaped cup of the whipped cream for decoration. Fold the remaining whipped cream into the pastry cream until smooth, then refrigerate.

Make sure your prepared layer cake bases are completely even in size. If not, trim to fit. To assemble, place the almond layer on a serving plate and spread a thin layer of raspberry jam/jelly on top. Add a third of the pastry cream mixture, and spread evenly. Repeat the cream and jam/jelly addition again with the first and second sponge cake layers.

Turn the third and final sponge cake layer over and add a thin, even layer of jam/jelly. Place it, jam side down, onto the pastry cream on the layer below. Ensure the whole cake is even and stable. Use a little of the leftover whipped cream and a spatula to even the filling around the edges so the sides are straight.

To make the icing/frosting, add the icing/confectioners' sugar to a bowl along with 1–2 tablespoons of hot water and mix until smooth. Add the warm, melted chocolate. If it is too thick, add a bit more water. Too thin, a bit more sugar. You want a smooth, thick yet spreadable consistency. Spread a generous layer on top of the cake to the edge.

Work the marzipan with a little icing/confectioners' sugar, then roll it out to a piece long enough to fit around the sides of the cake and the same height as the cake exactly. Do it in two lots if you find this easier.

Cut the edges of the marzipan so they are sharp, then wrap around the cake and secure with a dab of water. Put the reserved whipped cream in a piping/pastry bag and pipe dots of cream all around the top edge, hiding where the chocolate ends. Refrigerate before serving.

Verdens beste kake
WORLD'S BEST CAKE

Calling something the 'world's best cake' is quite a statement, but not something taken lightly by the Norwegians. This cake contains the most delicious whipped cream, sponge, pastry cream and meringue – it's everything you could ever want wrapped up together in one bite. This cake is so seriously good that it is often labelled the national cake of Norway. It is also known as *Kvæfjord* cake. Kvæfjord is a municipality in Tromsø in northern Norway, an absolutely stunning place with picture-perfect rolling green hills, rocky fells and deep blue *fjords*. To eat this cake in that setting: it doesn't get better than that, at least not in my mind.

150 g/1¼ sticks butter

130 g/²/₃ cup caster/granulated sugar

5 egg yolks

150 g/1 cup plus 2 tablespoons plain/all-purpose flour or cake flour

1 teaspoon baking powder

1 teaspoon vanilla sugar OR extract OR use the seeds from 1 vanilla pod/bean

100 ml/¹/₃ cup plus 1 tablespoon whole milk

FILLING:

150 ml/²/₃ cup whipping cream

¹/₂ portion of Pastry Cream (see page 14)

MERINGUE TOPPING:

5 egg whites

a pinch of cream of tartar

250 g/1¼ cups caster/granulated sugar

75 g/²/₃ cup flaked/slivered almonds

a 35 x 25-cm/14 x 9³/₄-inch rectangular cake pan, greased and lined with baking parchment

SERVES 8-10

Preheat the oven to 160°C (325°F) Gas 3.

In a stand mixer (or using a hand-held electric whisk) cream together the butter and sugar until pale and light. Add the egg yolks one at a time, beating to ensure everything is well incorporated. Sift in the plain/all-purpose or cake flour, baking powder and vanilla and fold in. Lastly, add the whole milk and fold again until fully combined. Spoon the mixture into the prepared pan and spread out evenly and set aside aside for a moment.

Next make the meringue topping. Using a completely clean bowl, whisk the egg whites with the cream of tartar until soft peaks form. Add the sugar very slowly, bit by bit, beating on high speed until stiff peaks form (about 5 minutes). Spread the meringue mixture on top of the cake mixture. Scatter the flaked/slivered almonds on top.

Bake in the preheated oven for 35–40 minutes or until a skewer inserted into the middle comes out clean and the meringue is firm. Leave to cool for a few minutes in the pan then turn out carefully, so the meringue is still on top. Leave to cool completely.

Whip the cream until stiff and fold together with the pastry cream.

To assemble, cut the cake into two halves. On one half, spread the pastry cream mixture, then carefully layer the other half on top. Leave to set in the refrigerator for an hour before serving. The meringue will stay mallowy and the base soft.

Looking across the morning mist on the fjords, waiting for the world to become clearer and lift itself out of darkness.

BREADS
& BATTERS

From soft buns to real flaky Danish pastries, there
is a huge tradition in Scandinavia for baking with sweet
yeasted dough. There is nothing cosier than watching
the world go by while making a batch of cinnamon buns.
Or for those days when you don't feel like something
sweet, make a batch of savoury waffles instead.

Spandauer wienerbrød
CUSTARD 'SPANDAU' PASTRIES

Spandauer pastries are named after Spandau, the Berlin borough, although they don't have anything to do with Germany – this pastry is as Danish as they come. In Denmark, these are most often made with either pastry cream or raspberry jam/jelly in the middle. They're nicknamed 'the baker's bad eye'. Not a very charming name, admittedly, but you can forgive it because they are so delicious. Try experimenting with different fillings such as cherries, blueberries or even apricots. At home, I often add rhubarb pieces on top of the custard.

1 portion of Danish Pastry Dough (see page 13)

1 portion of Remonce Almond Paste (see page 15)

¼ portion of Pastry Cream OR good-quality raspberry jam/jelly

1 beaten egg mixed with 1 tablespoon single/light cream, for brushing

2–3 tablespoons roughly chopped toasted hazelnuts

ICING/FROSTING:
100 g/¾ cup plus 1½ tablespoons icing/confectioners' sugar

1–2 tablespoons hot water

2 baking sheets, greased and lined with baking parchment

a piping/pastry bag fitted with a small plain nozzle/tip

MAKES 12–14

On a lightly floured surface, carefully roll out the Danish pastry dough and cut into 12–14 squares of around 10 x 10 cm/4 x 4 inches each.

Place a generous teaspoon of remonce almond paste into the middle of each pastry square, then carefully fold each of the 4 corners in to meet in the middle, using the sticky remonce to hold the corners down. Place the pastries on the prepared baking sheets, then cover with clingfilm/plastic wrap and set aside to rise for 20 minutes.

Preheat the oven to 200°C (400°F) Gas 6.

Brush the tops of each pastry with a little of the beaten egg and cream mixture. Add a teaspoon of your preferred filling (pastry cream OR jam/jelly) into the centre of each square. Lastly, add a sprinkling of chopped toasted hazelnuts to the centre, too.

Bake in the preheated oven for around 10–15 minutes or until golden brown, then remove and allow to cool before decorating.

To make the icing/frosting, mix the icing/confectioners' sugar with 1–2 tablespoons of hot water, adding more if needed. You are looking for the consistency of runny honey. Fill the piping/pastry bag and pipe a loose spiral of white icing/frosting around the edges of each pastry.

Note: Leftover bits of this pastry work very well to make the Romkugler (Rum Treats) on page 56.

Tebirkes
DANISH PASTRY POPPY SEED SQUARES

Ask any homesick Dane for the pastry that they simply cannot get outside Denmark, and
I bet you, *tebirkes* will be first on the list. There are two versions – the more savoury one (less
sugar in the dough and no filling) and then this slightly sweeter one with the remonce filling.
Up until the 1960s, only the more savoury variety was available, but a baker from Copenhagen
once had some leftover remonce, and this beautiful sweet version was born, it became known
as the *Copenhagener*. It does make such a decadent Sunday morning breakfast treat.

1 portion of Danish Pastry
Dough (see page 13)

1 portion of Remonce
Almond Paste (see page 15)

1 beaten egg mixed with
1 tablespoon single/light
cream, for brushing

100 g/^{2}/$_3$ cup poppy seeds

*2 baking sheets, greased and
lined with baking parchment*

MAKES 12

On a lightly floured surface, carefully roll out the Danish pastry dough
to a large square of around 40 x 40 cm/15^3/$_4$ x 15^3/$_4$ inches. Cut the
square in half and roll each half a little wider. Trim the edges straight.

Spread the remonce almond paste on ^{2}/$_3$ of each piece of dough
lengthways. Fold the 'naked' side towards the middle and the other
side on top of that so you end up with two long bits of pastry with
three layers each.

Slice each long piece into 6-7 portions, making sure that the slices are
nice and thick, around 5 x 6 cm/2 x 2^1/$_4$ inches. If the slices are too thin
the pastries may collapse when they bake. Cover with clingfilm/plastic
wrap and leave to rise for about 20 minutes.

Preheat the oven to 200°C (400°F) Gas 6.

Place the pastries on the prepared baking sheets and brush with
the beaten egg and cream mixture. Add a generous amount of poppy
seeds on top.

Bake in the preheated oven for around 10-15 minutes or until baked
through and golden-brown all over. The filling may seep out a bit
as it bakes so you may want to add a tray at the bottom of your oven
to catch any drips of melted butter. Remove from the oven and allow
to cool before eating.

Savoury variation: omit the remonce almond paste, and when cooled
slice open and serve with butter and cheese as a delicious savoury roll.

Semlekrans
SEMLA BUN WREATH

Every year on Shrove Tuesday before Lent, Scandinavians stuff their faces with these cream and marzipan-filled buns known as *semlor*. Baking them in a ring creates a lovely centrepiece.

25 g/1 oz. fresh yeast or 13 g/2^1/$_2$ teaspoons dried/active dry yeast

250 ml/1 cup whole milk, heated to 36–37°C (97–98°F)

80 g/^{3}/$_4$ stick butter, melted and cooled slightly

40 g/3^1/$_4$ tablespoons caster/granulated sugar

300–400 g/2–3 cups white strong/bread flour

^{1}/$_2$ teaspoon salt

1 teaspoon baking powder

2 teaspoons ground cardamom

1 egg, lightly beaten

FILLING:

100 g/3^1/$_2$ oz. good-quality store-bought marzipan (or see basic recipe on page 15)

a good dollop of Pastry Cream (see page 14)

500 ml/2 cups whipping cream

1 teaspoon vanilla sugar OR extract

icing/confectioners' sugar, to dust

a baking sheet greased and lined with baking parchment

a piping/pastry bag fitted with a star shaped nozzle/tip

MAKES A 9-BUN WREATH

If using fresh yeast, add it to the warm milk and mix until dissolved, then pour into the bowl of a stand mixer fitted with a dough hook. If using dried/active dry yeast, sprinkle the yeast granules into the warm milk and whisk together. Cover with clingfilm/plastic wrap and leave in a warm place for about 15 minutes to activate and become frothy and bubbly. Pour into the bowl of a stand mixer with a dough hook.

Stir in the melted butter, then stir in the sugar. Add half of the flour with the salt, baking powder and ground cardamom. Add half the beaten egg (reserve the other half for brushing before baking).

Mix well until all the ingredients are incorporated and then more flour, bit by bit, until you have a slightly sticky dough. Take care not to add too much flour. Knead the dough for at least 5 minutes in the stand mixer or 10 minutes by hand. Cover the bowl with a kitchen cloth and leave to rise in a warm place for 30–40 minutes or until doubled in size.

Turn the dough out onto a floured surface. Knead it through again, adding more flour if needed. You want a firmer but not dry dough. Split the dough into 9 equal portions and roll into round balls as neatly as possible. Place on the prepared baking sheet in a tidy circle, ensuring equal space of around 2.5 cm/1 inch between each bun. Cover with a kitchen cloth and leave to rise for a further 20 minutes.

Preheat the oven to 200°C (400°F) Gas 6.

Brush the wreath lightly with beaten egg, then bake in the preheated oven for 10–12 minutes or until golden and baked through. Remove from oven and immediately cover with a damp kitchen cloth.

Transfer the cooled bun wreath to your serving platter. Using a very sharp serrated knife, cut deep triangular holes into each bun and reserve the lids. Scoop out ^{1}/$_3$ of the inside and mix these crumbs with the marzipan and a good dollop of pastry cream to make the filling. Pipe the filling mixture into the hole in each bun.

Whip the whipping cream until stiff with a little icing/confectioners' sugar and vanilla sugar. Pipe even swirls of cream on top of the filling, on each bun. Place the 'lid' back on each bun – facing same direction – and dust lightly with icing/confectioners' sugar before serving.

Kanelbullar
REAL CINNAMON BUNS

Having a good recipe for *kanelbullar* is essential, because it's the Scandi treat you will make over and over. Don't forget to knead some love into the dough; it makes them extra-delicious.

DOUGH:

13 g/2¹/₂ teaspoons dried/active dry yeast or 25 g/1 oz. fresh yeast

250 ml/1 cup whole milk, heated to 36–37°C (97–99°F)

80 g/³/₄ stick butter, melted and cooled slightly

40 g/3 tablespoons caster/granulated sugar

400–500 g/3–3²/₃ cups white strong/bread flour

2 teaspoons ground cardamom

1 teaspoon salt

1 egg, beaten

FILLING:

80 g/¹/₂ stick plus 1 tablespoon butter, at room temperature

1 teaspoon plain/all-purpose flour

1 tablespoon ground cinnamon

¹/₂ teaspoon ground cardamom

¹/₂ teaspoon vanilla sugar

80 g/¹/₄ cup plus 2 tablespoons caster/granulated sugar

beaten egg, for brushing

TOPPING:

3 tablespoons golden/light corn syrup (warmed) and nibbed 'pearl' sugar

2 baking sheets, greased and lined with baking parchment

MAKES 16

If using fresh yeast, add the warm milk to a mixing bowl and add the yeast; stir until dissolved, then pour into the bowl of the food mixer. If using dried/active dry yeast, pour the warm milk into a bowl, sprinkle in the yeast and whisk together. Cover with clingfilm/plastic wrap and leave in a warm place for about 15 minutes to become bubbly. Pour into the bowl of a food mixer fitted with a dough hook.

Mix in the cooled, melted butter. Allow to combine for 1 minute or so, then add the sugar. In a separate bowl, weigh out 400 g/3 cups of the flour, add the cardamom and salt and mix. Start adding the flour and spices into the milk mixture, bit by bit. Add half the beaten egg. Keep kneading for 5 minutes. You may need to add more flour – you want the mixture to end up a bit sticky. It is better not to add too much flour as this will result in dry buns. You can always add more later.

Cover the dough with clingfilm/plastic wrap. Allow to rise for around 30 minutes or until it has doubled in size.

Turn the dough out onto a lightly floured surface. Knead through with your hands and work in more flour if needed. Roll out the dough to a 40 x 50 cm/16 x 20 inch rectangle.

In a bowl, add the butter, flour, spices and sugars and mix together well to make the filling. Using a spatula, spread the mixture evenly over the rolled-out dough. Fold the dough in half lengthways.

Using a knife or pizza cutter, cut 16 widthways strips of dough. Take one strip and carefully twist it a few times, then curl into a 'knot', ensuring both ends are tucked in or under so they do not spring open during baking. Place the folded 'knots' on the prepared baking sheets spaced well apart. Leave to rise under a kitchen cloth for 30 minutes.

Preheat the oven to 200°C (400°F) Gas 6.

Brush each bun lightly with beaten egg and place in the preheated oven to bake for around 10–12 minutes or until golden.

Remove from the oven. Brush the warm buns lightly with syrup then decorate with the nibbed 'pearl' sugar. Immediately cover with a damp, clean cloth for a few minutes to prevent the buns from going dry.

Sallys chokladbullar
SALLY'S CHOCOLATE BUNS

I love to make fun variations of the everyday *fika* bun. These delicious chocolate buns come from our Sally at the café, who makes them at home when she fancies something different from the usual cinnamon bun. We felt that just using chocolate spread doesn't work because it burns easily, but mixing it to a paste with some extra chocolate helps make the most indulgent and chocolatey buns possible. These are pretty hard to resist, for kids and adults.

1 portion of Real Cinnamon Bun dough (see page 149)

FILLING:
50 g/3^1/2 tablespoons butter, softened

75 g/^{1}/3 cup plus 2 teaspoons light brown soft sugar

4 large heaped tablespoons chocolate hazelnut spread (such as Nutella)

1 tablespoon plain/all-purpose flour

50 g/2 oz. good-quality milk/semisweet chocolate, chopped (I use Lindt or Marabou)

beaten egg, for brushing

2-3 tablespoons golden/light corn or date syrup

a generous handful of toasted hazelnuts, roughly chopped

a baking pan with sides, greased and lined with baking parchment

MAKES 16

Prepare the dough as directed on page 149 and leave to rise.

In a food processor or stand mixer, combine the butter, light brown soft sugar, chocolate hazelnut spread and flour and blend until you have a smooth, spreadable mixture. Set aside.

Turn the dough out onto a lightly floured surface and knead it through. Roll the dough out to a large rectangle of around 30 x 40 cm/11^3/4 x 16 inches.

Spread the chocolate filling in an even layer across the dough. Scatter with the chopped milk/semisweet chocolate.

Roll the dough up tightly lengthways to form a long sausage, then cut into 16 even pieces using a knife or pizza cutter.

Squash the buns tightly together into the prepared baking pan if you would prefer a traybake to tear and share (pictured). Or if you want to make individual buns then space them spread out evenly on two larger baking sheets. Cover with a kitchen cloth and leave to rise for a further 20 minutes.

Preheat the oven to 200°C (400°F) Gas 6.

Brush the buns with a little beaten egg, then bake in the preheated oven for around 8-10 minutes or until golden brown. Remove the buns from the oven, then brush immediately with the golden/light corn or date syrup. Decorate each bun with toasted chopped hazelnuts.

Immediately place a damp, clean kitchen cloth on top for a few minutes to prevent the buns from going dry.

Fødselsdagsboller
BIRTHDAY BUNS

My *farmor* (grandmother) Inger used to bake these for us on birthdays and treat days. After running around in the cold getting rosy cheeks, we'd head back into the warm house for one of these sweet buns. We'd eat them with so much butter our teeth would leave an indent (this phenomenon is known as *tandsmør* – literally meaning tooth butter!). In Denmark, these birthday buns are traditionally arranged in the shape of a stick man or woman, then baked and decorated with icing and wine gum mouths, liquorice eyes and gummy laces for hair.

200 ml/³/₄ cup whole milk

50 ml/3¹/₂ tablespoons single/light cream

25 g/1 oz. fresh yeast or 13 g/2¹/₂ teaspoons dried/active/dry yeast

50 g/¹/₄ cup caster/granulated sugar

400 g/3 cups white strong/bread flour

1 teaspooon salt

1 egg

80 g/³/₄ stick butter, softened

beaten egg, for brushing

a baking sheet, greased and lined with baking parchment

MAKES 12

Mix together the milk and cream and heat to finger-warm (around 36–37°C/97–98°F).

If using fresh yeast, add the yeast and warmed milk-cream to a stand mixer with a dough hook attached. Mix until the yeast has dissolved. If using dried/active dry yeast pour the warmed milk and cream into a bowl. Sprinkle on the yeast and whisk together. Cover with clingfilm/plastic wrap and leave in a warm place for about 15 minutes to activate and become frothy. Pour into the stand mixer with a dough hook.

Add the caster/granulated sugar and stir again, slowly adding half the flour mixed with the salt, bit by bit. Add the egg and softened butter and keep mixing. Slowly add the other half of the flour. You may not need all the flour or you may need a bit more, but keep mixing until you have a slightly sticky dough that is starting to let go of the sides of the bowl. This should take around 5–7 minutes.

Cover the bowl with clingfilm/plastic wrap and leave to rise for around 35–40 minutes or until doubled in size.

Turn the dough out onto a lightly floured surface and knead through with your hands, adding only a little more flour if needed.

Cut the dough into 12 equal pieces and roll them into uniformly round balls. Place on the prepared baking tray. Cover again and leave to rise for a further 20 minutes.

Preheat the oven to 200°C (400°F) Gas 6.

Brush each bun lightly with beaten egg, then bake in the preheated oven for around 10–12 minutes or until golden brown.

Remove from the oven and place a damp, clean kitchen cloth on top for a few minutes if you prefer the buns without a hard crust. Serve sliced open, with butter or some Scandinavian sliced cheese.

Smørkage
BUTTER CAKE

Smør means butter in all the Scandinavian languages – we are butter-loving nations!
Smørkage literally means butter cake, two of my favourite words of all time, married together.

25 g/1 oz. fresh yeast or
13 g/2¹/₂ teaspoons dried/
active dry yeast

150 ml/²/₃ cup whole milk,
heated to 36–37°C
(97–98°F)

2 tablespoons caster/
granulated sugar

1 egg

350–400 g/2¹/₂–3 cups
white strong/bread flour

¹/₂ teaspoon salt

¹/₂ teaspoon ground
cardamom

150 g/1¹/₄ sticks butter,
softened and cubed

FILLING:

¹/₂ portion of Pastry Cream
(see page 14)

1 portion of Remonce
Almond Paste (see page 15),
but made with half soft dark
brown sugar, half caster/
granulated sugar in place
of the icing/confectioners'

50 g/¹/₄ cup raisins

beaten egg, for brushing

25 g/¹/₄ cup flaked/slivered
almonds

TOPPING:

50 g/¹/₃ cup icing/
confectioners' sugar

1 tablespoon cocoa powder

*a 26-cm/10¹/₄-inch
springform/springclip or
round cake pan, greased and
lined with baking parchment*

SERVES 8

If using fresh yeast, add the yeast and warm milk to a stand mixer with a dough hook attached. Mix until the yeast has dissolved. If using dried/active dry yeast, pour the warm milk into a bowl. Sprinkle on the yeast and whisk together. Cover with clingfilm/plastic wrap and leave in a warm place for about 15 minutes to activate and become frothy and bubbly. Pour into the stand mixer with a dough hook attached.

Add the caster/granulated sugar and egg and mix again at medium speed. Start to add some of the flour, along with the salt and cardamom. Add the butter, at this stage mixing it in alternatively with bits of the flour. Stop adding flour once you have a fairly soft dough – you can always add more later. Cover the bowl with clingfilm/plastic wrap and leave in a warm place for about 40 minutes to rise.

Turn the dough out onto a lightly floured surface and knead through. Set two thirds of the dough aside. Roll the one third out into a circle that will fit into the cake pan. Spread on a layer of remonce almond paste, then a generous, even layer of pastry cream to cover the dough (you may not need it all). Add the raisins and put the pan to one side.

Roll out the remaining two thirds dough to a 30 x 30 cm/11³/₄ x 11³/₄ inch square and add the rest of the remonce filling, spreading evenly. Roll the dough up into a tight roll and cut into 8 equal swirls. Place one swirl in the middle of the pan on top of the pastry cream and the rest around it, evenly. Squash the swirls down a bit if needed. Cover the pan with clingfilm/plastic wrap then leave to rise for another 25 minutes.

Preheat the oven to 180°C (350°F) Gas 4.

Brush the cake with beaten egg, scatter over the flaked/slivered almonds and bake in the preheated oven for around 20 minutes. After this time, cover the top with foil and turn the heat down by about 20°C/70°F. Bake for another 20 minutes or until cooked. Remove from the oven and immediately cover with a clean, damp kitchen cloth to prevent a crust from forming. Leave to cool before serving.

To make the topping, sift together the icing/confectioners' sugar and cocoa powder and stir with a few spoons of hot water until smooth. Swirl over the cake and leave to set. This cake does not keep very well so is best served the same day it is made.

Æbleskiver
DANISH CHRISTMAS PANCAKES

Go to any Danish household in December, and you are likely to be served these little treats. The word *æble* means apple, and these are traditionally baked with a little piece of apple inside. In my family, we don't add apple, but you of course can. These are so lovely they feature in my house all year round – and I sometimes serve them at breakfast with sausage and scrambled egg, too. Sorry, Mum. I know it's wrong, but it's so good!

3 eggs, separated

300 ml/1¼ cups buttermilk

100 ml/⅓ cup double/heavy cream

1 teaspoon vanilla extract

1 tablespoon caster/granulated sugar

½ teaspoon salt

1 teaspoon baking powder

½ teaspoon bicarbonate of/baking soda

1 teaspoon ground cardamom

250 g/1¾ cups plus 1 tablespoon plain/all-purpose flour

grated zest of 1 medium lemon (or to taste)

50g/3½ tablespoons butter, melted for frying

icing/confectioners' sugar, for dusting

raspberry jam/jelly, for dipping (optional)

an æbleskive pan, Japanese takoyaki pan or frying pan/skillet

MAKES 30

Mix together the egg yolks, buttermilk, double/heavy cream and vanilla extract in a large mixing bowl. In a separate bowl, sift together all the dry ingredients including the cardamom.

In another clean bowl, whisk the egg whites until stiff using a hand-held electric whisk on high speed.

Add the egg and cream mixture to the dry ingredients, then carefully fold in the beaten egg whites and lemon zest. Leave to rest for 30 minutes in the refrigerator before using.

Place the pan over high heat to warm through and add a little melted butter to the pan to stop the pancakes from sticking. If you are using an æbleskive pan, carefully add enough batter to each hole so that it reaches about 0.25 cm/⅛ inch from the top. If you are using a normal frying pan, add spoonfuls of batter as you would if making normal small pancakes. Leave to cook for a few minutes until the edges become firm then, using a fork or knitting needle (knitting needle is easier!), gently turn the pancakes over to cook on the other side. If you have filled the holes too much, this can be tricky - you'll get the hang of it after a few.

Once browned on both sides (3–4 minutes per batch), keep the cooked æbleskiver warm in the oven until you have finished frying.

Serve dusted with icing/confectioners' sugar and a little pot of raspberry jam/jelly for dipping.

For the love of baking

One of my earliest memories is sitting in my *farmor* Inger's warm kitchen. I remember her kneading dough for me and my sister to make *boller* (buns). I recall the warmth of her kitchen and the smell of spices. I remember trying to make lots of different shapes of bun and brushing them with egg wash. Impatiently watching them rise, then waiting for them to bake, pacing backwards and forwards by the oven door...

Finally, when my grandmother took the buns out of the oven, she let us split them open and spread them with butter, which melted on the warm fluffy surface. The taste was out of this world and at that moment I knew I loved baking. To this day, with every batch of bread I make, I hope to have this same feeling of delight.

Many of our dearest childhood memories are associated with food. The taste of ice cream on the beach on a summer's day, the picnics, the birthday cakes, the hot chocolates on cold days.

Sometimes, just a taste of the same flavour of ice cream can transport us back in an instant to a moment in time. The memories we develop through the foods we make and eat as children are incredibly powerful. At the café, where a lot of customers are ex-pat Scandinavians living in London, I often tell people that my job is to provide a temporary remedy for homesickness. Scandinavians seek out a specific brand of chocolate or a particular cake, so that they can be instantly transported back home just for a few moments.

The food we make and share in our homes with the people we love creates so many important memories in our lives, and I truly believe that what we learn in the kitchen helps shape us as people. The art of cooking and baking teaches us about everything, from the science of the ingredients to patience. For me, the kitchen was – and still is – a place where we talk, we learn, we connect and we love. We *hygge*.

I know I'm very lucky: the amount of love in the kitchens I grew up in is unfathomable. I try to make sure that both my kitchens – at home and in the café – are full of the same warmth. Teaching my children to make recipes from their heritage is how I teach them about where they come from. There is no subject we can't discuss when we bake. Scandinavians have a long tradition of home baking and we have a sweet tooth generally, but we also understand how to balance it by making sure that it's home-baking – not mass-produced stuff – that wins out.

In my family, we are both home cooks and bakers. My great-grandfather was a trained *Konditor* in Denmark and he met my great-grandmother as they worked in a restaurant where she was making open sandwiches. In my home, my husband Jonas teaches our kids to cook and create, and I get to be the Mamma who is always happy to bake a batch of buns.

I'm not a trained baker. I'm a cook who runs and owns a café in London with a mission to bring simple Scandinavian food to everyone. I am also a mother. First and foremost I am a lover of sweet things, of spices and of warm ovens. We hope you enjoy our book full of authentic Nordic treats – it was created with love in my warm kitchen during the dark autumn and winter months of the year, with help from two eager little girls called Astrid and Elsa, who love cracking eggs and testing warm cakes as they come out of the oven. And so the circle is complete.

Munkki
FINNISH DOUGHNUTS

Did the Finns invent the doughnut? Perhaps not, but the Finnish version of doughnuts – known as *munkki* – are absolutely delicious. They have been an integral part of Finnish baking culture for generations and are especially popular around Walpurgis Night. In Swedish, these doughnuts are called *munk ringar* (monk rings), which refers to the iconic hairline of the monks. My friend Maija and her mother Tuula have been so kind as to share their family recipe.

25 g/1 oz. fresh yeast or 13 g/2½ teaspoons dried/active dried yeast

250 ml/1 cup plus 1 tablespoon whole milk heated to 36–37°C (97–98°F)

30 g/2½ tablespoons caster/granulated sugar

400–500 g/3–3¾ cups plain/all-purpose flour, plus extra for kneading

½ teaspoon salt

1 teaspoon ground cardamom

50 g/3½ tablespoons melted butter

1 egg, beaten

1 teaspoon lemon juice

1 litre/34 fl oz. vegetable oil, for deep-frying

granulated sugar or cinnamon sugar (mixed at a 1:5 ratio), to coat

a cook's thermometer

MAKES ABOUT 20

If using fresh yeast, add the yeast and milk to a mixer with a dough hook attached. Mix until the yeast has dissolved. If using dried/active dry yeast pour the milk into a bowl. Sprinkle over the yeast and whisk together. Cover with clingfilm/plastic wrap and leave in a warm place for about 15 minutes to activate and become frothy and bubbly. Pour into the mixer with a dough hook attached.

Add the sugar and mix with the dough hook until dissolved. Combine the flour, salt and cardamom and start to add to the mixer bit by bit. Pause adding flour when the dough begins to stick and add the butter, egg and lemon juice. Continue again to add the flour until you have a firm yet sticky dough. Be careful not to add too much flour at this stage or the doughnuts will be dry.

Cover the bowl with clingfilm/plastic wrap and leave the dough in a warm place to rise for about 30–35 minutes or until doubled in size.

Turn out the dough onto a lightly floured surface and knead it through. Add a little more flour if needed. Portion off a piece of the dough and roll it into a small sausage of about finger thickness. Join the ends together to make little rings of around 5–6 cm/2–2½ inches in diameter, leaving a good sized hole in the middle. Scatter more flour on a surface and place the rings there as you go along.

Cover the dough rings with a kitchen cloth and leave to rise for a further 30 minutes.

Heat the vegetable oil in a deep-fat fryer or large, deep saucepan to 180°C (350°F). Carefully test a doughnut in the hot oil. It should need between 1–2 minutes each side to turn light golden-brown all over.

Cook the doughnuts in batches then remove and drain on paper towels before rolling in cinnamon sugar (or just granulated sugar, if preferred) to coat. Eat on day of making. **Tip:** You can also make round doughnuts and pipe them full of raspberry jam/jelly or pastry cream (see page 14).

Frasvåfflor
CRISPY SWEET WAFFLES

In our first book, we gave you a recipe for a breakfast waffle. You may think that a waffle is just a waffle – but there are different types. These ones are called *frasvåfflor* and are crispier, best eaten straight away with a dollop of jam or sticky vanilla syrup and fresh fruit. You'll find this type of waffle served in most huts on the *fjells* where people go to ski. This recipe is from my mother-in-law, Eva. She makes these for us when we visit their house in Sälen in Sweden. After spending the precious daylight hours in the snow on the mountains where they live, we'll get back to the cottage and warm up in front of the log fire. Then we all gather at the table to eat freshly made *frasvåfflor.*

150 g/1¼ sticks butter, melted, plus a little extra for greasing

300 g/2¼ cups plain/all-purpose flour

2 teaspoons baking powder

1 teaspoon vanilla sugar OR extract OR use the seeds from 1 vanilla pod/bean

250 ml/1 cup plus 1 tablespoon whole milk

250 ml/1 cup plus 1 tablespoon water

cloudberry or strawberry jam/jelly and whipped cream, OR vanilla bean syrup and fresh fruit to serve (optional)

a heart-shaped waffle iron – available online. You can use a different shaped iron, but cooking time and yield may vary

MAKES 16

Heat up the waffle iron and brush with melted butter.
Mix all the ingredients (apart from the serving suggestions) together to form a smooth batter.

Add a ladle full of batter to the preheated waffle iron and close the lid. Leave to cook for 2–3 minutes or until golden brown and crispy. Remove and serve immediately with plenty of cloudberry or strawberry jam/jelly and whipped cream. Repeat with remaining batter.

Vanilla bean syrup: To make a quick vanilla bean syrup to serve with the waffles, combine 150 g/¾ cup caster/granulated sugar with the seeds from 1 vanilla pod/bean and 100 ml/⅓ cup water. Bring to the boil then simmer for 4–5 minutes over high heat, taking care not to let the mixture bubble over or the sugar burn. If it's reducing too quickly, shorten the cooking time or you will end up with a syrup that's too thick. Remove from the heat and add sea-salt flakes to taste. Pour over the waffles to serve.

Västerbottensvåfflor
Med spenat

VÄSTERBOTTEN AND SPINACH WAFFLES

On one of those days where only an abundance of cheese will do, you will find me hogging all the *Västerbotten* to myself – it's such a delicious Swedish cheese. I make these waffles on cold winter days when the rain and sleet forces us to cosy up inside. This is the perfect low-effort snack – just throw everything together and cook in the waffle iron. Jonas, my husband, loves the bacon/pancetta pieces in these waffles – but you can omit if preferred.

100 g/1 stick minus 1 tablespoon butter, melted, plus extra for greasing

150 g/1 cup plain/all-purpose flour

75 g/$\frac{1}{2}$ cup wholegrain spelt flour

2 teaspoons baking powder

75 g/$\frac{3}{4}$ cup finely grated Västerbotten cheese (or mature/sharp Cheddar)

100 g/$\frac{1}{2}$ cup blanched, cooked spinach, or 3–4 frozen balls (defrosted), liquid squeezed out and chopped

a pinch of salt

freshly ground black pepper

150 g/1$\frac{1}{2}$ cups chopped, cooked smoked bacon pieces/pancetta

sour cream, to serve (optional)

a heart-shaped waffle iron – available online. You can use a different shaped iron, but cooking time and yield may vary

MAKES 7–8

Heat up the waffle iron and brush with melted butter.

Combine all the ingredients (apart from the sour cream) together with 350 ml/1$\frac{1}{2}$ cups water and stir to incorporate and form a smooth, thick batter.

Add a ladle of batter to the hot waffle iron. Close the lid and cook for 2–3 minutes or until golden brown.

Remove from the pan and serve immediately with sour cream.

Knäckebröd
HOMEMADE CRISPBREAD

In Scandinavia, crispbread is not a diet bread – it just happens to be healthy and delicious. It has been a staple on our lunch tables since way back when Harald Bluetooth was a nipper.

25 g/1 oz. fresh yeast or 13 g/2¹⁄₂ teaspoons dried/active dry yeast (note: you can also make this with a sourdough starter, but you'll need to try with your own starter to see what quantity works for you)

250 ml/1 cup milk heated to 36–37°C (97–98°F)

2 tablespoons runny honey OR bread syrup OR corn syrup

150 g/1 cup wholemeal/wholegrain rye flour

300–400 g/2¹⁄₄–3 cups light rye flour (type 997)

2 teaspoons salt

50–75 g/¹⁄₄–¹⁄₂ cup seeds, spices or toppings of your choice (I sometimes use pumpkin seeds, poppy seeds or sunflower seeds. For stronger flavours, I use cumin, caraway or fennel seeds. You can even add cinnamon for a festive feel)

2–4 large baking sheets, greased and lined with baking parchment or a large pizza stone

**MAKES 8 LARGE
OR 16 SMALL**

If using fresh yeast, add the yeast and warm milk to a stand mixer with a dough hook attached. Mix until the yeast has dissolved. If using dried/active dry yeast pour the warm milk into a bowl, sprinkle over the yeast and whisk together. Cover with clingfilm/plastic wrap and leave in a warm place for about 15 minutes to activate and become frothy and bubbly. Pour into the mixer with a dough hook attached.

Add the honey or syrup and stir again. Sift together the flours and salt and add to the mixture. Continue to mix with the dough hook for at least 5 minutes on medium speed. The dough needs to be firm but if it is too dry and crumbly then mix in a few tablespoons of water.

Cover the bowl with clingfilm/plastic wrap and leave the dough to rest for around an hour in a warm place. It will not rise much, but should puff up a little.

Preheat the oven to 220°C (425°F) Gas 7. Add a pizza stone to the oven if you have one handy (this speeds up the cooking).

Turn the dough out onto a lightly floured surface and gently knead it through. Split into 8 large or 16 smaller pieces. Roll each piece of dough into a ball, then roll out each onto a piece of baking parchment until really thin or around a millimetre in thickness. Arrange on the baking sheets. Add your chosen seeds or toppings, pushing them into the dough slightly. Brush with water and prick liberally with a fork all over. I like my cripsbread salty, so I usually also add a spinkle of salt flakes at this stage too. I also usually cut a hole in the middle of mine, but this is just for show. If preparing in batches, keep the dough covered with a kitchen cloth to prevent it from drying out.

Bake in the preheated oven for 4–8 minutes or until slightly browned and firm. If you are not using a pizza stone, you may need to turn the cripsbread over midway through cooking.

Remove from the oven and allow to cool on the trays. Once the oven has cooled to just warm, pop the crispbread back in to finish drying. Enjoy with sliced meats, pâtés, smoked fish or grated Västerbotten cheese mixed with crème fraîche and cream cheese, spiked with extra pepper and topped with cloudberry jam/jelly.

Svenska scones
SWEDISH SCONES

Baking bread at home doesn't have to take ages. I often make these Swedish scones if I don't have bread in the house, they take just a few minutes to put together and not long to bake. Swedes refer to these as *Svenska* scones, but the basis for them is actually more akin to making soda bread, rather than the traditional English scone for afternoon tea. This recipe is quite forgiving – you can vary the flour you use to suit your taste (although if you use lots of rye or coarse wholemeal/wholegrain, you will need to add a bit of extra liquid or plain flour). I also sometimes add seeds or even grated carrots to the mixture. These scones are delicious served with plenty of butter and maybe a slice of mild Scandinavian cheese.

200 g/$1^1/2$ cups wholemeal/wholegrain spelt flour

250 g/$1^3/4$ cups plus 2 tablespoons plain/all-purpose flour

4 teaspoons baking powder

1 teaspoon salt

125 g/$1^1/8$ sticks butter, cubed

200 ml/$^3/4$ cup whole milk

150 g/$^3/4$ cup Greek yogurt, skyr or filmjölk or similar soured or strained milk

1 tablespoon golden/light corn syrup

beaten egg or milk, for brushing

2 baking sheets, greased and lined with baking parchment

MAKES 16

Preheat the oven to 200°C (400°F) Gas 6.

In a bowl, combine the flours, baking powder and salt. Mix in the cubed butter with your hands until the mixture is grainy and even.

Add the milk, yogurt and syrup and combine with the flour and butter. Mix lightly until you have an even, grainy dough. Don't knead it.

Cut the dough into 4 even pieces and roll each one into a ball. Flatten the balls to discs of around 15–16 cm/6–$6^1/4$ inches in diameter. Cut a cross almost all the way through on each disc.

Arrange on the prepared baking sheets and brush with beaten egg or milk. Bake in the preheated oven for 15–18 minutes or until golden brown, well-risen and baked through. Leave to cool slightly before breaking each disc into 4 along the scored lines.

Slice open to serve. Best eaten on day of baking.

Rågkakor
RYE FLAT ROLLS

These light rye flat rolls are so super-soft that my kids refer to them as 'pillow bread' –
and always ask for them in their packed lunches (they freeze well too). Traditionally, these are
made with *rågsikt* (*sigtemel*) – a flour blend of 40% sifted rye flour and 60% white bread flour.
Don't use dark rye for these rolls, it will not work – you need to get the lighter rye.

50 g/3 tablespoons fresh
yeast or 25 g/1 oz. dried/
active dry yeast

300 ml/1^{1}/$_4$ cups water
heated to 36–37°C/97–98°F

300 ml/1^{1}/$_4$ cups whole milk,
heated to 36–37°C/97–98°F

50 g/^{1}/$_4$ cup golden/light
corn syrup

50 g/3^{1}/$_2$ tablespoons
butter, melted

200 g/1^{1}/$_2$ cups light rye
flour (type 997), sifted

1 teaspoon salt

550 g/4 cups white strong/
bread flour (or more if
needed)

100 g/^{3}/$_4$ cup oatmeal/
rolled/old-fashioned oats
(run larger oats through the
food processor to make
them finer)

*2–4 large baking sheets,
greased and lined with
baking parchment*

*3 cm/1^{1}/$_4$ inches or
2 cm/^{3}/$_4$ inch round pastry/
cookie cutter*

**MAKES 4 LARGE
OR 8 SMALL**

If using fresh yeast, add the yeast, milk and water to a stand mixer
with a dough hook attached. Mix until the yeast has dissolved. If using
dried/active dry yeast, pour the warm milk and warm water into a
bowl. Sprinkle over the yeast and whisk together. Cover with clingfilm/
plastic wrap and leave in a warm place for 15 minutes to activate and
become frothy and bubbly. Pour into the mixer with a dough hook.

Add the golden/light corn syrup and melted butter and stir again. Add
the rye flour, salt and half of the white flour and mix with the dough
hook until fully incorporated. Add the oatmeal. Continue adding white
flour and knead for around 4–5 minutes until you have a slightly sticky
mixture that is coming together and letting go of the sides of the bowl.

Place the dough in a clean lightly oiled bowl and cover with clingfilm/
plastic wrap. Leave in warm place to rise for about 45 minutes or until
doubled in size.

Turn out the dough onto a lightly floured work surface. Knead through,
then split into 4 or 8 equal parts and shape into balls. If you are making
4 large rolls, roll out the balls into circles measuring about 20–25 cm/
8–10 inches in diameter. If you are making 8 smaller rolls, roll into
circles measuring about 10 x 12.5 cm/4 x 5 inches. The rolls should be
thin, at around 1 cm/^{3}/$_8$ inch thick.

Place the rolls on the prepared baking sheets. Cut a hole in the middle
of each with the appropriate size pastry/cookie cutter, cover and leave
to rise for a further 20 minutes.

Preheat the oven to 200°C (400°F) Gas 6.

Prick the breads evenly all over with a fork, all the way to the base.
Bake in the preheated oven for around 10–12 minutes or until lightly
browned and risen. Cooking times may vary – if you are making large
rolls they will take a little longer than the small ones.

Remove from the oven and immediately cover with a damp kitchen
cloth to prevent a crust from forming. Serve either sliced in half
as sandwiches or as they are, with toppings.

INDEX

ACKNOWLEDGMENTS

Thank you to my daughters: chief cake tester Astrid Aurell and chief egg cracker Elsa Aurell; and to my extremely patient husband Jonas. I could not have written this book without you guys. Love you always.

Ryland, Peters & Small – especially Julia, Cindy, Sonya, Alice and Maria. To the brilliant team who worked so hard on the beautiful photography in this book: Pete, Tony, Bridget, Jack, Laura, Casey and Lola.

To my agent, Jane Graham Maw and our PR team at Samphire.

All our wonderful colleagues at ScandiKitchen: Rebekka, Martina, Thom, Torben, Marta, Roxanne, Luke, Sally, Karin, Valdemar, Hanna, Nanna, Alexandra, Christina, Karoly, Paula, Livia, Felicia, Caroline, Malin, Tina, Richard, Peter, David Cross and The Lord of the Ledger David Holberton.

Our amazing families back in Denmark and Sweden: the Blomhøjs and the Aurells. Thanks for your love, support, feedback and recipes.

David Jørgensen and Andy McLaughlin for always having red pens and kind words handy, at any given hour.

Friends, testers, left-over cake eaters, general support and sanity: Sandra and Chad (who have yet to refuse a bun). Laura Thomson, Theresa Boden, Helle Kaiser-Nielsen, Birgitte Agger Mote, Karen Nash, Maija Hansen, Sheena Skinner, Andrew Robertson, Hannah Ventura, Sarah Hand, Jennifer Hadley, Ida Jonsson Gahnström, Marianne Jenkins, Michelle Sirkett, Jenny Linford, Barbro & Duncan McAusland, Laura Leaver and Louise Wisson.

The Danish ladies who baked their way through a ton of cake: Karin Chessell, Maria Dumas, Marie Knoebelauch, Kir Rathje Belhocine, Jette Rayner, Veronika Stjernevang, Katrine Bavnbek, Pia Rathje-Burton, Mette Geddes, Pernille Schulz, Stephanie Bock, Mia Møller, Danielle Sharpling, Jeanette Steinbeck, Katja Schneekloth, Benedikte Moffat, Mette Lindahl-Wise, Mette Poynton, Birthe Vejby Nielsen, Lone Friis, Pia Nielsen, Bette Petersen Broyd, Irene Rughave Rumens, Ingrid Somnier, Tilde Valentin, Mia Austin, Rikke Christensen, Mette Theilman, Nina Marie Fuglesang, Jeanette Winther Andersen, Jane Nielsen, AnnaMarie Gray, Berrit Christine Boje Vilstrup, Signe Damtoft, Heidi Christensen, Linnea Ploen, Christina Kjolner, Pernille Thomsen and Natasja Jones.

The biggest thank you of all to our wonderful customers at the café who pop by and see us, and those who contact us from all corners of the world – you guys make what we do worth it, and we are humbled to share our journey with you.

Thank you.

Ryland Peters & Small would also like to thank Blåbär – Nordic Living for loaning us their beautiful items to be photographed.
www.blabar.london